New Findings on
Shirdi Sai Baba

This book is based on in-depth research that triangulates information from several primary sources, to provide hitherto unknown facts about Sai Baba, village Shirdi and some of the people who visited it during the late 19th and early 20th centuries. It not only adds to the repository of knowledge about this great saint of India and the role that he played in the context of protecting his devotees during India's struggle for freedom, but additionally provides new insights by raising questions and seeking answers through analysis of rare documents drawn from the National Archives, police records and diaries pertaining to that time as well as reviewing personal documents and literature in different languages. It contains nine chapters dealing with different aspects of Sai Baba's life in Shirdi.

The book has several rare documents and photographs of Shirdi Sai Baba and his devotees as well as compositions of Shirdi of that time. A glossary is provided at the end of the book for ease of reference.

The book will be a valuable asset not just for all those who are devotees of Sai Baba and other Sadgurus, but also for students and academics who have an interest in India's culture and history and in the means used by the British to understand and control developments in different parts of the country.

गुरुर्ब्रह्मा गुरुर्विष्णुगुरुर्देवो महेश्वर:।
गुरु: साक्षात्परब्रह्म तस्मै श्रीगुरवे नम:॥

New Findings on
Shirdi Sai Baba

Dr. C.B. Satpathy

STERLING PAPERBACKS
An imprint of
Sterling Publishers (P) Ltd.
Regd. Office: A1/256 Safdarjung Enclave,
New Delhi-110029. CIN: U22110DL1964PTC211907
Tel: 26387070, 26386209
E-mail: mail@sterlingpublishers.in
www.sterlingpublishers.in

New Findings on Shirdi Sai Baba
© 2019, Dr. C.B. Satpathy
ISBN 978 93 86245 52 6

Printed and Published in India by

Sterling Publishers Pvt. Ltd.,
Plot No. 13, Ecotech-III, Greater Noida - 201306, U. P. India

Preface

With the spread of Sai consciousness across the globe and the increasing number of temples and related activities carrying on in the name of Shri Sai Baba of Shirdi, it is desirable that the devotees and others understand Shri Sai Baba and his philosophy in a proper perspective. This book aims to portray certain aspects related to Shri Sai Baba when he was in Sagun form and thereafter.

My earlier books on Shri Sai Baba describe him from a devotee's view, based on faith and personal experience. However, this book strives to provide an objective and evidence-based narrative about him instead. This is not an easy task. It is quite tough to establish the plausible as the possible. A jump from faith to reasoning is one of the most difficult tasks that any believer can face.

Since long, numerous postulates and hypotheses on aspects of Shri Sai Baba that are shrouded in mystery, are afloat. There is inadequate verifiable information regarding his parentage, place of birth, caste, religion and early childhood. Similarly, divergent views exist about the date on which he first arrived at Shirdi and his age at that time. While some argue that he first came to Shirdi in 1854, others consider this event to be about eighteen years later in 1872. A number of such unanswered questions propelled me to undertake an in-depth research to try and seek evidence-based answers. The search for records and documents took my research team and me to the National Archives at Delhi and Kolkata, the Indian Museum, Kolkata, a number of libraries in Maharashtra and many other places. Some references were found even from the British Library, London.

My personal interaction with the descendants of devotees who had a direct link with Shri Sai Baba, like Udhav Baba, son of Shama of Shirdi; Shivamma Tai of Bangalore; Shivesh Swamy and many others, between 1990 and 1995, were extremely useful in my quest.

In order to learn about the view of the Imperial British Government of India about Shri Sai Baba, the relevant official documents, particularly of the Police, Revenue and Criminal Intelligence Departments of that time, were extensively reviewed. Primary sources of evidence and data, from hitherto unexplored sources were very useful. Such data include the three weekly intelligence reports from the local units of the Directorate of Criminal Intelligence (D.C.I.), Ahmednagar district and sent to the D.C.I. Headquarters, Kolkata. During the colonial regime, the Home Department of the Government of India received political and criminal intelligence reports through the D.C.I., which was headed by a British officer usually belonging to the I.C.S. (Indian Civil Service).

Thus, the nine chapters contained in this book are mostly based on primary evidence to the extent possible.

The earliest literature available on Shri Sai Baba was by Dasganu Maharaj, who was a police constable and a kirtankar. He wrote books entitled *Bhakta Leelamrit, Santa Kathamrit* and *Bhakta Saramrit*. Subsequently, scores of persons wrote many books in most of the Indian languages and some foreign languages as well. Many of these have been published by the Shri Saibaba Sansthan Trust, Shirdi. Not only the prominent Indian writers like B.V. Narasimha Swami, M.V. Kamath, Indira Kher, V. B. Kher and others, but also many foreign writers like Antonio Rigopoulos, Kevin R.D. Shepherd, Arthur Osborne, Marianne Warren, Karline McLain and others have written numerous books on Shri Sai Baba. Above all, Govind Raghunath Dabholkar's book *Shri Sai Satcharita* has become universally accepted and regarded as a pothi or scripture by the Sai devotees.

Some of the books focus on various aspects of Shri Sai Baba, like his arrival in Shirdi, dealings with the devotees, sayings and philosophy, daily routine at Shirdi, miracles performed by him, environment of Shirdi around him, religious, social and philanthropic activities around him and the socio-religious impact of Shri Sai Baba, then and now. Scanning the abundant literature on Shri Sai Baba we can easily discern a certain amount of repetitiveness of anecdotes and themes, where miracles of Shri Sai Baba are mostly highlighted. The language used in many of the books appears to be somewhat similar and replete with oriental hyperboles, which at times cloud the exactitude of the basic theme and events. Nevertheless, the valuable contribution of these writers cannot be understated. As a step forward, this book ventures to further explore some important aspects relating to Shri Sai Baba which were either hitherto unknown or not explained fully.

One of the main objectives of this book is to generate among the readers, writers and researchers a spirit of research and to motivate them to undertake intensive research on the life, deeds and philosophy of Shri Sai Baba. It is written in a style and manner suitable for the devotees as well as the academics and intellectuals. It is desirable that Indian universities, especially those of Maharashtra, undertake research on Shri Sai Baba and related matters. Emphasis on the universities of Maharashtra is laid because many of the documents relating to Shri Sai Baba are in Marathi or Modi language.

It is important to note that any study on Shri Sai Baba's personality and noble deeds would require the formulation of a system which would use a combination of methods that are used for historical, autobiographical, religious and spiritual research. This is required because a lot of opinion and perception, based on assumption and hearsay, have slowly crept into his hagiography. Obscurantism is not good, even in the path of religious belief. Adopting a scientific approach to understanding Shri Sai Baba and the Sai Path will be valuable in adding to the body of existing knowledge for the future of humankind.

*****

Acknowledgements

I have been immensely helped by many persons in the creation of the manuscript over the last two-and-a-half years. Mrs. Neha Sikka Arora and Mr. Sachin Sikka have been painstakingly correcting my written material from the very beginning, a large number of times. They have collected material, photographs and sketches from numerous sources and re-framed and composed them. Bharti Raina, a student of Delhi University has been assisting in the correction of the manuscript.

At my behest, over the last four years, Mr. Vivek Gupta and his wife Mrs. Anu Gupta visited places like Mumbai, Pune, Aurangabad and Shirdi to meet persons whose forefathers were directly connected with Shri Sai Baba. They collected valuable information, documents and photographs from them and also translated information from Marathi to Hindi. Similarly, Mr. Arun Kaushik and Mrs. Madhu Kaushik have been extremely helpful in collecting information and relevant documents from the National Archives, Delhi and many other museums and archives. Mr. Jitender Shelke of Shirdi helped me in collection of some vital documents written in Marathi and Modi language. Besides, discussions with Mr. Pramod Aher of Shirdi regarding some of the issues raised in the book, were useful.

Mrs. Varsha Tarkhad has been immensely helpful in translating some important material from Marathi to English. Both Mr. Abhishek Satpathy and Mrs. Asima Satpathy have provided timely support in this venture when it was needed, in various ways.

Some of my well-wishers like Mr. A.R. Nanda, I.A.S. (Retd.) and Mr. S.C. Panda, I.A.S. (Retd.), who have also written books on Shri Sai Baba, have rendered valuable suggestions. Mr. R.C. Joshi, I.A.S., has also been associated with the creation of manuscript.

Others, who from time to time, have rendered various types of help in this work, are Ms. Kumkum Bhatia, Mr. Saurabh Vatsa, Mr. Snehasish Ray, Mr. Devendra Singh Negi and Mr. Debabrata Satpathy.

Having created the draft manuscript, a person of high academic excellence was needed to edit the manuscript and format it. I could have found no person better than Dr. (Mrs.) Aasha Kapur Mehta, former Professor of Economics, I.I.P.A., Delhi. She is the editor of the tri-monthly magazine the *Heritage of Shirdi Sai*. I have no words to express my gratitude towards her meticulous contribution in the formatting and editing of the manuscript.

The initial drafts of three chapters were read and corrected by my son Arunabh Satpathy, M.S. in Management Information Systems, University of Washington, USA. My wife Meera and daughters Shweta and Trishna kept on encouraging me to complete the book as soon as possible. I received great help from the family members.

Finally, I would like to thank Shri Surinder Kumar Ghai, the Managing Director of Sterling Publishers Pvt. Ltd., New Delhi, in taking due care towards the publication of this book.

Introduction: Shri Sai Baba

Shri Sai Baba of Shirdi is a well-known spiritual personality of India. Today, his name and fame have travelled beyond India to countries across the globe. His religious and philanthropic activities and philosophy are observed by all his followers. His parentage, place of birth, caste, religion, early childhood and date of arrival at Shirdi are shrouded in mystery. The only established fact is that after settling for a few decades in Shirdi, an unknown village of the Central Provinces of British India, he left his body on 15th October 1918. After his departure, known as "Mahasamadhi" in Hindu parlance, his property and the Samadhi Mandir where his body is entombed, were taken over by the Shri Saibaba Sansthan Trust, Shirdi, formed in 1922. Presently, the Trust is ensuring the continuation of the daily worship routine of Shri Sai Baba and taking care of the comforts of the devotees and visitors from India and abroad. Reportedly, an average of about sixty thousand people visit Shirdi each day.

Shri Sai Baba of Shirdi has been accepted and heralded as a Sadguru, that is, a spiritual mentor, by his devotees and an avatar or incarnation by most. Some people have tried to associate him with the Sufi sect, others with the Dattatreya sect, yet others with the Vaishnavite sect or Shaivite sect, or even the Avadhoot sect of the Navanaths, though, he cannot be straightjacketed into any of these and goes beyond them. He is addressed by his devotees as Baba, Sai Baba, Shri Sai Baba, Shri Sainath Maharaj, Sai Mauli and by many more epithets. He has also been connected with various deities of the Hindu pantheon, like Ganapati, by various devotees. All this reflects the high spiritual esteem in which Shri Sai Baba is held by them.

Shri Sai Baba's personality, as can be gauged by his activities at Shirdi, did not reflect that he was a religious personality of a classical pattern. His approach towards the spiritual evolution of his devotees was unique and, at times, unconventional. Usually, he did not preach abstract philosophy or ethics in a didactic fashion. Nevertheless, he spelt out the ethical standards when discussing various issues with his devotees. He did not resort to demagogy or pedagogy to influence the devotees and also the public. He behaved spontaneously and naturally with all. His main concern was the qualitative evolution of the mind, leading to pious activities. Essentially, Shri Sai Baba stood for humanitarianism, cutting across the barriers of caste, creed, religion, language and temporal differentiation between individuals. In this way he encouraged social reform. He had an unbiased approach towards his devotees, whether they were big persons or small. He prescribed simple living, universal kinship, mutual tolerance, a spirit of sacrifice and a balanced code of conduct in family and social life. His philosophy is less reflected through his sayings and more through the saintly activities that he performed. Although he was visited by rich and poor, happy and distressed, educated and uneducated devotees, he treated all of them in the same manner. He was not only a lover of human beings but also of the animals around him. He was a spiritual leader, a social reformer and a protector of his devotees. For all the support and benefits he gave everyone and anyone who approached him, he never sought any material returns. He only wanted them to evolve in life and live a happy life.

As a result of his multi-dimensional activities – both temporal and spiritual – for the amelioration of his proteges, music, literature, folklore, drama and even some amount of gossip filled the social environment of the village. It is said that "not a leaf moves without his desire". That is what used to happen at Shirdi. Be it the construction of a temple or a house, the sickness of an individual, the spread of cholera in the village, the education or rearing of children, the celebration of any religious or social festival, or the settlement of conflict, Shri Sai Baba's word was the final expression of wisdom and judgment. He stood between his devotees and suffering. Most of the villagers and the visiting populace willingly followed this way of living with Shri Sai Baba. Those who failed to do so experienced that any deviation from such practices and procedures, even if not obligatory, became a risky adventure.

A study of the books written by different authors, both Indian and Western, including *Shri Sai Satcharita* leads to the conclusion that the activities of Shri Sai Baba at Shirdi were multi-dimensional and hyper kinetic. He was virtually the un-throned king of Shirdi, affecting the lives of hundreds of people.

The last two decades have witnessed an exponential growth in the number of devotees of Shri Sai Baba and related activities, like building of temples, educational institutions, healthcare institutions and others. Numerous books exclusively dedicated to Shri Sai Baba, written in most of the Indian languages and some foreign languages including English, are available. These books mostly deal with the life, pious activities and philosophy of Shri Sai Baba. A large number of e-magazines can also be seen.

During the year 2017-2018, the activities pertaining to Shri Sai Baba have proliferated and magnified. The centenary year of his Mahasamadhi has become a pious occasion for the devotees and Shri Sai Baba related institutions to create centenary events, inaugurate temples, schools and hospitals and to conduct multiple humanitarian activities.

There is a substantial increase in the number of foreign nationals who visit Shirdi from across the world. In order to cater to the needs of the devotees, an airport has been opened in Shirdi recently. In response to the growing needs of Shri Sai Baba's devotees who travel from all parts of India to worship him, a number of additional trains to Shirdi have been commissioned by the Ministry of Railways.

The same is the case with the growth in journals, magazines, books and other literature about him. A lot of philanthropic, charitable and religious activities are undertaken by various trusts and temples created in Shri Sai Baba's name. We can find volumes of information about Shri Sai Baba through different websites dedicated to him on the internet. Given, the trajectory of its exponential growth, the Sai movement is bound to soar to greater heights in future.

*****

Contents

List of Photographs

List of Tables

Shri Sai Baba's Mahasamadhi

This chapter provides details regarding the highly auspicious day on which Shri Sai Baba took Mahasamadhi; his wish to be taken to the wada; donation to Laxmibai, his dream commands to continue his aarti; his last rites, puja and sandal procession by Hindus and Muslims; prior indications to devotees about his crossing over the ocean of worldly life; narration by two devotees about his last moments; and formation of a committee.

The Highly Auspicious Day on Which Shri Sai Baba Crossed Over the Ocean of Worldly Life

Shri Sai Baba took Mahasamadhi on Tuesday, 15th October 1918, a highly auspicious day in both the Hindu and Muslim calendars. It was the ninth day of Ramzan and it also happened to be the major Hindu festival of Vijayadashami. Furthermore, Ekadasi had just started. The significance of the date and time of Sai Baba's Mahasamadhi are listed in table 1.1 based on information reported in *Shri Sai Leela*.

Table 1.1: The significance of the date and time at which Shri Sai Baba took Mahasamadhi

English Date	15 October 1918, Tuesday
Marathi Date	Ashwin Shukl 11 Shaka 1840
Muslim Date	9 Mohorram Hijri San 1337
Parsi Date	5 Ardi Behast San 1227
Time of Maha Nirvana	Afternoon 2:35 (East Kal – Exactly 21 Ghati)
Nakshatra, Charan	Dhanishta Nakshatra 2nd Charan
Yoga, Karan, Ritu	Shul, Gar, Dakshinayan, Sharad Ritu

Source – *Shri Sai Leela* (1983: 23)

Shri Sai Satcharita mentions about Sai Baba's Mahasamadhi as follows:

> Baba got a slight fever on 28th September, 1918. The fever lasted for 2 or 3 days, but afterwards Baba gave up his food, and thereby grew weaker and weaker. On the 17th day, i.e., Tuesday, the 15th October, 1918, Baba left His mortal coil at about 2.30 p.m.
>
> Gunaji 2002: 220

Yet another publication, *Sainath Prabha*, published in October 1918 (photograph 1.1), mentions that:

> Shri Samarth Sainath Maharaj took Samadhi last Tuesday i.e. Ashwin Shukl 10 at 3 in the afternoon. Around 5-6 days prior to his Mahasamadhi, he stopped his daily routine like walking up to Lendi, going to Chawadi, going for Alms and conversing with people. Tuesday, that is the same day as Samadhi day, in the morning, got a vision, "I am here, haven't gone, perform the Kakad aarti, get up." After the afternoon aarti, everyone in the Masjid were asked to leave for their places for lunch. Sai Baba left his body around 3 in the afternoon. At that time, there were only 2 or 3 devotees with Baba, rest all went to their houses. He left his body at the place where he usually used to sit with his elbows on the railing. It is decided to keep his Samadhi in the building built by Bapusaheb Buti.
>
> *Sainath Prabha* Kiran 10, 1918:
> Shri Samarth Sainath Maharaj Prasann, self-translated

This seems to be accurate in view of the fact that an inscription behind the wooden door leading to the Samadhi Mandir mentions that Sai Baba left his mortal body in the Dwarkamayi at about three o'clock on 15th October 1918.

Moments before his passing away, Sai Baba's last words to Bayaji Appa Kote Patil and Laxmibai were to take him to the wada.

Photograph 1.1: *Sainath Prabha* Kiran 10th October 1918

To Appaji he said, *"Mee jato mereku wadaku uchlun de sagale brahmana majuya jabalu rahteel"* (Swami 2006: 170).

[I am going. Carry me to wada. All Brahmins will be living near me.]

And to Laxmibai, after giving her nine rupees and before leaving his body, his words were, *"Are ata malaa ithe vare vaatat naahi, vaanyat gheyun chala manjhe vare vaatel"* (*Shri Sai Leela* Issue 11, 1923: 79).

[Here I am not feeling well now, take me to the wada, I will feel better.]

> While saying these words, He leaned on Bayaji's body and breathed His last. Bhagoji noticed that, His breathing had stopped, and he immediately told this to Nanasaheb Nimonkar, who was sitting near. Nanasaheb brought some water and poured it in Baba's mouth. It came out. Then, he cried out loudly "Oh Deva!" Baba seemed to open His eyes and say "Ah" in a low tone. But it soon became evident that, Baba had left His mortal body for good.
>
> Gunaji 2002: 226

A different version of his last moments as recounted by a teacher in Shirdi, Usha Prabhakar Mule, is in an article published in *Shri Sai Leela* in 1983 – more than six decades after Sai Baba's Mahasamadhi. It is based on information she received from Bappaji Laxmanrao Ratnaparkhi, a resident of Shirdi. According to his recollection, Sai Baba suffered due to fever from 3rd October and was in pain till 14th October 1918. On 15th October, as usual, he went to Lendi for the toilet, brushed his teeth, washed his hands and sat next to the pillar opposite the Dhuni. After some time, he went to his Devalya place. As usual he recounted stories on Brahma gyan and then asked for an early aarti. Jog and his wife performed Sai Baba's puja and offered naivedya. After distributing Udi to all those who were present, he asked them to go to Dixit wada for lunch. It was approximately 1.30 p.m. at that time. Sai Baba asked Mhadu Fasle to make a pan beeda, which he placed on Sai Baba's hand and gave water from the silver jhaari. Sai Baba tried to sip a little water but half of it came out. He then slowly rested himself on the shoulders of Bayaji Kote, who was sitting behind him, and then gave nine coins to Laxmibai. Through this, he conveyed that he had followed the paramarthic tradition of donation at the time of death.

By 2.30 p.m., his situation worsened and seeing his failing health, the five people present, namely, Bayaji Kote, Bhagoji Shinde, Laxmibai Shinde, Mhadu Fasle and Bappaji Ratnaparkhi, rushed to Dixit wada, conveyed the situation and brought Dr. Chidambaram Pillay Nagpurkar back with them. The doctor took Sai Baba's hand and checked his pulse and observed that the atma of Shirdi had merged in Universe (Mule 1983).[1]

The day after Sai Baba's Mahasamadhi, at sunrise, Sai Baba appeared in Das Ganu's dream at Pandharpur saying:

> The mosque has tumbled down. All the grocers and oil-merchants of Shirdi have harassed me. So I am now going away from there. Hence, I have come up to here. Cover me up in an abundance of flowers. O, do fulfil this wish of mine! Come! Come immediately to Shirdi!
>
> Kher 2014: 696

Laxman Mama Joshi, on receiving a dream command from Sai Baba, "Get up soon, Bapusaheb thinks that, I am dead and so he won't come, you do the worship and the Kakad (morning) a[a]rti!" (Gunaji 2002: 227), arrived at the appropriate time and performed the aarti of Sai Baba in the Dwarkamayi Masjid on the morning of 16th October 1918. Then, in the afternoon, Bapusaheb Jog and others performed the aarti which also took place in the Masjid, as usual (Gunaji 2002: 227; *Shri Sai Leela* Issue 6 1923: 54).

Devotees Flock to Shirdi on Hearing about Shri Sai Baba's Passing Away

The news about the passing away of Sai Baba spread like wild fire in Shirdi and the nearby villages by word-of-mouth. In those days, use of telephone or even telegraph was a rare event. Postal mail was the fastest source of communication.

One of the earliest news items on Sai Baba's Mahasamadhi was published in the Pune edition of the famous newspaper *Kesari* on 22nd October 1918 on page 6 under the column "Vartmansaar" (photograph 1.2).

The news said:

> Shri Sadguru Sainath Maharaj on Tuesday 15th October laid his body to rest and his Samadhi is located in Shri Gopal Rao Mukund Buti wada. Sunday 27th is a day for Bhandara, all devotees of Maharaj to come, as informed by Rev Hari Sitaram Dikshit.
>
> Newspaper *Kesari*, self-translated

Photograph 1.2: Newspaper *Kesari* 22nd October 1918: Bhandara on thirteenth day on 27th October 1918 as informed by H.S. Dixit

This news of Sai Baba's taking Mahasamadhi spread rapidly and within no time thousands came to Dwarkamayi for a final darshan, queuing for five or six hours.

A photo of Sai Baba was published in the obituary in *Sainath Prabha* in November 1918 (photograph 1.3).

श्रीसाईनाथ महाराज.

ता॰ १५ आक्टोबर रोजी समाधिस्थ झाले.

सूचना.

ज्या वर्गणीदारांकडून अद्याप वर्गणी आली नाहीं, त्यांजकडे पुढील १२ वा अंक धरी पाठविण्यांत येईल तरी तो त्यांनी स्वीकारण्याची मेहेरबानी करावी.

Photograph 1.3: *Sainath Prabha* Kiran 11th November 1918, Obituary

Puja and Sandal Procession by Hindu and Muslim Devotees

Both Hindus and Muslims venerated Sai Baba and so both conducted his last rites in their own way. Bappaji Laxmanrao Ratnaparkhi, who was in Shirdi at that time, described the pujas and sandal procession to Mule as follows:

> Baba's thirteenth-day function was held as per Hindu traditions organized by Mumbai based devotees, which included Kakasaheb Dixit, Kaka Mahajani, Moreshwar Rao Pradhan, Tarkhad, Sundarrao Navalkar, Govind Rao from Pune, Rasne Kaka, Khagjiwale. Boondi ladoos were distributed as prasad by them. Seeing all this appeared as a day of jatra. Huge crowds gathered for prasad. Thirteen Brahmins conducted the puja. Each of the Brahmins was offered a dhoti, shawl and dakshina of Rs. 21. This puja was performed by Kakasaheb Dixit; Shri Balasaheb Deo was also present there. Sandal procession was carried out by Muslim devotees on the evening of 20th day and was followed by reading of Quran and Namaz prayer.
>
> On the 40th day, Dasganu performed a 3-day puja festival. One thousand devotees were fed food. Pandit Shastriji from Pandharpur was invited for the puja. Brahmins were offered silver pela (tumbler) and clothes. One such pela is still with Ratnaparkhi.
>
> On the 60th day, Shri Upasani Maharaj went to Kashi and performed hawan as per Vedic rituals and gave alms or donations. Like this the Mahanirvan puja was completed. However, the Light is still present here in invisible form.
>
> *Shri Sai Leela* 1983: 27[2], self-translated

Prior Indications to Devotees about Shri Sai Baba Crossing Over the Ocean of Worldly Life

Sai Baba gave several indications about his Mahasamadhi in different ways. Some of these are outlined here.

- Two months earlier, Sai Baba sent a message to fakir Banne Mia Fakir, saying that:

  Navdin, nav tarikh: Allah meyane apna dhunia le jayega, merji Allaki.

Shri Sai Leela 2007: 47

[Ninth day, Allah himself takes away the lamp which Allah has placed.] *Navdin nav tarikh* meant ninth day of the ninth month. Sai Baba's passing away was actually on the ninth day of the ninth month.

- He also sent some offerings to the fakir Shamsuddin Mia with a request to do two types of devotional singing called moula (vocal singing of songs about God) and kowali (beating of the table and singing songs about saints). He also requested nyas, that is, preparing food and feeding the people (Swami 1994c: 174–175).

Thus, right until the final moments of his body, Sai Baba was embracing both Hindu and Muslim communities.

- In 1916, at the time of Shilangan and Dussehra day, Sai Baba had indicated the importance of Vijayadashami for crossing over the "border of the ocean of worldly life" by hinting that for this "Dussehra is the only auspicious time" (Kher 2004: 694). While he told Ramchandra Patil (Kote) that "in the year 1918, in the month of Ashwin (October) during the sun's southerly passage, on the Vijayadashami day, in the bright half of the moon, Tatya will go to his Eternal Abode" (Ibid).

When the month of Ashwin began, Tatya was bedridden and suffered high fever. He was "unable to walk or move about" and the "illness was taking a turn for the worse. . . . Then came dashmi . . . the pulse grew feeble as Tatya lay dying" (Ibid: 695).

However,

The danger to Tatya's life was averted. Tatya remained while Baba it was, who passed away, as if in exchange for Tatya! And see the marvel of Baba's words! He took Tatya's name, but was really making ready for his own niryan, without missing the exact time, even by a second. And yet he had given the warning, bringing to the notice of all, the future event. But until it happened actually, no one had realised it.

Ibid: 696

• Sai Baba also appeared in the dream of Mrs. Pradhan who lived in Santacruz, Mumbai giving her intimation about his Mahasamadhi.

On 16-10-1918, i.e. the night after Baba's departure, I saw his body in a dying condition in my dream and said "Baba is dying". Baba replied, "People do not talk of saints as dying, but as taking Samadhi." His body was still. People were mourning. Such was the dream. I felt sad. I woke at 12.30 midnight. In the morning we got from Anna Chinchnikar, a card that Baba passed away at 3 p.m., on Dusseraha 15-10-1918.

Swami 2006: 110

• Some days before his departure:

There occured an ominous sign foreboding the event. There was, in the Masjid, an old brick on which Baba rested His hand and sat. At night time. He leaned against it and had His Asan. This went on for many years. One day, during Baba's absence a boy who was sweeping the floor, took it up in his hand, and unfortunately it slipped and fell down and broke into two pieces. When Baba came to know about this, He bemoaned its loss, saying: "It is not the brick, but My fate, that has been broken into pieces. It was my life-long companion, with it I always meditated on the Self, it was as dear to Me as My life, it has left Me to day."

Gunaji 2002: 228

• Similarly, it is a practice among Hindus, that when a person is about to die, religious scriptures are read out to him in order to help him get detached from the worldly things. Sai Baba, as he knew that he was about to pass away soon, asked one Mr. Vaze to read a book named Ramvijay to him. Mr. Vaze used to read the book once in the week. Then, Sai Baba asked him to read it again, day and night. Vaze completed reading the book, for the second time in three days. Thus, eleven days passed like this. He read it again for three days and hence got exhausted. Then, Sai Baba let him go and did not say anything after that. He then abided in his own self, waiting for the last moment to arrive (Gunaji 2009: 225).

Shri Sai Baba's Final Journey: Interment in Buti Wada

After a few hours, the question arose regarding what to do with Sai Baba's mortal remains. Some Muslims, including a Muslim butcher of Bandra, Mumbai, requested that the body of Sai Baba be kept in Samadhi, outside the mosque in the open space, outside Lendibagh (Gokhale 2004: 64). Khushal Chand and Amir Shakkar also supported this along with Shama. However, the village officer, Ramchandra Patil, who headed the group, insisted and took a firm decision that Sai Baba's last words be respected and that he be buried in Buti wada only. Discussions regarding this went on.

At that time Kakasaheb Dixit became upset and asked all those present to collect two lakhs of rupees for the temple construction. He requested them that in case they wanted the Samadhi to be made outside, they should sign documents as an assurance for donation of the money. No one expected this suggestion and, therefore, bickering followed among everyone. Seeing the state of confusion, Kakasaheb Dixit sent a telegram to the Collector of Ahmednagar to render help and solve the problem. Accordingly, Shri Sane, the local Mamlatdar, was ordered to handle this issue.

So, the Mamlatdar himself passed such an order, and Baba's body was buried without any difficulty at But[i] wada, where it still remains. That was only a temporary settlement. The more important matter was as to the guidance of the future. That should be a scheme sanctioned by the District Court of Ahmednagar. H.S. Dixit, with his remarkable legal ability, his worldly wisdom, and great bhakti, drew up a scheme and presented it with the signatures of a number of influential devotees. That was sanctioned by the District Court in 1922 and that governs the Shirdi Sai Sansthan and [Sai] Baba's tomb and other affairs. The property of the Sansthan [was] vested in a body of trustees with a managing committee of fifteen, Dixit contented himself with being the Honorary Secretary, and his able management pleased all the parties. H.S. Dixit thus laid firm foundation for the success of the Shirdi Sai Sansthan, and he must be given the credit for its present position.

Swami 1994b: 176

Since Sai Baba had expired intestate, examination of his body and writing of panchanama was conducted by Santaji Patel Shelke, the Police Patil of Shirdi. Shri Sane also took possession on all articles left behind by Sai Baba. Thereafter, Sane put to vote the issue of taking Sai Baba to Buti wada or to an open graveyard. The result showed that 1,503 voted in favour of Buti wada and 730 were in favour of an open graveyard. Ramchandra Patil, who was an active participant in this vote, reportedly conveyed this to the writer of Nirvanicha Sakha in 1964. Finally, paying due respect to Sai Baba's last words, it was decided that Sai Baba's body would be taken to Buti wada.

Sai Baba's body was wrapped in a white cloth and kept at Dwarkamayi (Gokhale 2004: 66–67). Even after thirty-six hours of his Mahasamadhi, Sai Baba's body had not turned stiff but was flexible as if he was alive (Gunaji 2002: 227).

Before entombing him, Sai Baba's mortal body was given a bath, incense was applied, a garland was offered and aarti was performed. It was a very intense and solemn time for the devotees that time. A mournful and solemn procession went around the village. People flocked everywhere and threw flowers and coins. Everybody took part in Baba's last procession. Bhajan mandali, horse, palki, rath all were part of the procession. Flowers, dakshina, gulal were offered. Certain articles like Satka, a chillum, needle and thread, brick were kept inside the Samadhi along with Baba's body. Tulsi, a black colo[u]red Tilak, Chandan, Kapur, perfumed flowers and scented liquid incense were applied. The work of burying Baba's body started.

Gokhale 2004: 66–67, self-translated

Balasaheb Bhate had the great honour of performing the last rites of Sai Baba after his Mahasamadhi. On the thirteenth day, he collected Brahmins from the village and began the last rites. The rituals of tilanjali, tiltarpan and pindapradan were also performed by Balasaheb Bhate (Kher 2004: 731–732; Nimbalkar 2004: 63).

Shri Sai Baba's Last Moments: Narration by Two Devotees

A beautiful narration about the last moments of Sai Baba and the reason for his entombment in Buti wada can be found in a letter written by G.G. Narke and published in *Shri Sai Leela*.

Bapusaheb, Kakasaheb and few others used to have their lunch with Sai Baba in the Masjid but on Tuesday 15th October, after Madhyaan Aarti, Baba sent all of them to their houses to have their lunch and during this time, Baba left this world.

At that time, Laxmi Bai (Patil), Bayaji, Bhagoji, Bala Shimpi, Laxman, Nanasaheb Nimonkar and others were there in the Masjid. Madhav Rao Deshpande was sitting on the stairs. Sai Baba gave some rupees (rupee 9) to Lakshmi Bai Patil, from His pocket and said after some time that "अरे अता मला इथे वरे वाटत नाही, वाण्यात घेऊन चला मंझे वरे वाटेल" (Here I am not feeling well now, take me to wada, I will feel better). Baba used to call Buti's wada as Dagdi wada or wada. This were his last orders and so it happened like that.

As per Shree's words to take Him to wada, everyone decided to keep Shree's body at Bapusaheb Buti's wada. Accordingly, the digging work for Shree's Samadhi started at the sanctum sanctorum of the temple. By evening, Rahata's Fouzdaar, etc. also arrived and the decision of Samadhi was firmed up. Shree's Samadhi was erected at the place where Gopal Krishna Murti was to come. The digging of this solid sanctum sanctorum continued throughout the night. Next day, a small disruption took place. In the morning, Amir Bhai from Mumbai and Kopargaon's Mamledar arrived at the scene. There was some dispute. Some people argued to take Shree outside to a field. Mamledar took votes and verdict of 2-1 was in favour of Shree's Samadhi at Shree Bapusaheb's Wada. Mamledar wanted to hand over this entire affair to Nagar's Collector, therefore Kakasaheb Dixit was ready to go to Nagar. Meanwhile, with Shree's grace, those initially opposed to the move also followed the majority decision. With full consensus, it was decided to have Shree's Samadhi in Bapusaheb's wada. On Wednesday evening, on Ekadasi day, Shree's body was taken to the sanctum sanctorum of the wada's temple in a procession. . . . Shree was always saying that He will be staying in this wada. . . . Just 4-5 days ago before passing away, Shree called Soni's mother and told her that, "आता मला मशीदीचा कंटाळा आला, चावडीचा कंटाळा आला, आता मी वड्यात जाऊन बसेन तेथे भेटलोक माझा सांभाळ करतील" (I am frustrated with Masjid, frustrated with Chawadi. I will go and stay in the wada where Brahmins will take care of me). 4-5 years ago, Baba showed this place to Jog's wife while holding her hand and said that this sanitation place belongs to me. Here a stone building will come where I will stay. (ही हगदोडीची जागा माझी आहे।इथे दगड़ी इमारत होईल। तेथे मी बसेन।). It seemed that Shree Samarth had already decided but he never let anybody know of it.

Humbly yours,
Ganpati Narke

Shri Sai Leela Issue 11, 1923: 78, self-translated

A statement of Gajanan Jaydev, who was also known as Appasaheb Chidambur, published in *Shri Sai Leela* says that shortly before his Mahasamadhi, Sai Baba told him to go home and let him sleep:

Shri Sai Baba left his body on Dussehra. That day, after the afternoon aarti, everyone left for their home and Baba told me, *"Tu ata ghari jha, mala jopayeche"* [You go to your home and let me sleep].

While saying this Baba covered his body with a white cloth and laid down. I went home. At four in the afternoon, a turmoil took place in the village and a huge crowd started to gather around the masjid. It was reported that Baba had left his body. The news that Baba had gone, spread like a quick-fire in the village. My parents did not allow me to go outside.

After sometime, Baba's death procession took place. A vehicle of four or six tires having four square shaped arms was brought for the procession. A circular cover was put and a clean white cloth was placed over it. As the vehicle was being pushed along the path, the whole village was lamenting. People from the neighbouring villages had come to attend this procession. The population of Shirdi wasn't much but at that time all the lanes were flooded with people. My parents too went out and saw the whole scene. But I had headed far and saw the vehicle for myself. . . . As I had gone too far, it took me a long time to reach back home. On reaching late, my father got angry and started to beat me. This was because, he thought that I might have made a contact with an untouchable and hence, I was again given a bath with hot water.

The procession party went through the major paths of the village and halted at the Sai Baba mandir, presently the Samadhi Mandir. Baba had told Mr. Buti of Nagpur to construct the temple and install the idol of Shri Vithal.

Just like Baba had instructed about the installation of the idol of Shri Vithal, it is believed that whenever Baba used to go out of the village, the walk being a morning ritual, he used to indicate and say to anyone nearby, *"Mee galayanantar ithe rahnar aahe"* [After my departure, I will stay here].

That's why the people of Shirdi agreed on making the temple the Samadhi place of Baba.

Shri Sai Leela Issue 12, 1988: 8, self-translated

Given all this information, we can summarize it in the following manner:

- Sai Baba's Mahasamadhi was on Tuesday, 15th October 1918. This was an extremely auspicious day for both Hindus and Muslims due to the combined occurrence of Vijayadashami, the ninth day of the month of Ramzan and Ekadasi.

- While some documents mention the time of his Mahasamadhi as 2.30 p.m. and 2.35 p.m., one document that was published shortly after his Mahasamadhi in October 1918 itself, reported it to be 3 p.m. This also seems to be accurate because the inscription behind the door leading to the Samadhi Mandir mentions 3 p.m. as the time of Sai leaving his mortal body. In any case, the difference between the two times is only half an hour, which is not significant.

- However, for our purposes what is important is that Ekadasi had begun and both Vijayadashami and the ninth day of Ramzan occurred on the day of the Mahasamadhi. These facts are important because Sai Baba regarded Vijayadashami as extremely auspicious for seemolangan or crossing over the ocean of worldly life. Further, Ramzan is the holy month of introspection for Muslims. Also, importantly, the alignment of the stars and planets on Ekadasi, is such that it is easier for the onward journey of the soul. Many of Sai Baba's closest devotees passed away on Ekadasi.

- Sai Baba's last words to Bayaji Appa Kote Patil and Laxmibai were to take him to the wada. He gave nine rupees to Laxmibai.

- However, we cannot state with certainty whether or not he was able to conduct his routine activities on the day of his Mahasamadhi. One document from October 1918 states that around 5-6 days prior to his Mahasamadhi, Sai Baba stopped his daily routine like walking up to Lendi, going to Chawadi, going for alms and conversing with people. However, there are other versions according to which even on the day of his Mahasamadhi, Sai Baba went for his daily chores as usual.

- The difference could be because when people looked back over time and tried to recount what happened, some of the points were not so clear in their memory.

- Several devotees located near and far received visions about Sai Baba's Mahasamadhi and were drawn to Shirdi.

- After Sai Baba's Mahasamadhi, Laxman Mama Joshi received a direct command in his dream from Sai Baba that he was not dead and his worship should continue. Hence, Laxman Mama did the morning aarti on 16th October 1918, after which the usual pattern of worship has continued till date.

- Both Hindus and Muslims venerated Sai Baba and so both conducted his last rites through pujas and sandal procession. Thus, up to his final moments as well as thereafter, Sai Baba embraced both communities.

- The Collector and District Magistrate, Ahmednagar, was intimated about the death of Sai Baba of Shirdi. With the support of the district authorities, Sai Baba's property was handed to the committee which had been formed to conduct the worship of Sai Baba's tomb. Thus, a firm foundation was laid for the success of the Shri Saibaba Sansthan Trust, which will be discussed later in this book.

Formation of the Shri Sainath Sansthan Committee

As mentioned earlier, Kakasaheb Dixit had mentioned in his letter dated 22nd October 1918 to the Collector and District Magistrate, Ahmednagar, about the death of Sai Baba of Shirdi and requested his property be handed to the committee which had been formed to conduct the worship of the Sai Baba's tomb (Annexure-1).

> On behalf of and as directed by the Shri Sainath Sansthan Committee I beg to inform you with deep regrets that His Holiness Shri Sai Baba of Shirdi breathed His last on Tuesday the 15th instant. His remains were pursuant to His wishes buried in the stately wada which Shrimant Gopalrao Mukund Buti commenced building under the orders of His Holiness and which is still under construction. . . . As the shrine will be a permanent institution it was deemed necessary to have a body to manage the same and the undermentioned persons were accordingly constituted into a Committee for the purpose of managing the said institution. . . . The names and descriptions of the persons constituting the Sai-committee are as under:

1. Shrimant G.M. Buti, a very rich Banker of Nagpur who has settled down at Shirdi and proprietor of the wada where the said shrine is located, President of the Committee now constituted as aforesaid.

2. Mr. Narayan Govind Chandorkar, retired Deputy Collector.

3. Rao Bahadur Hari Vinayak Sathe, retired Superintendent of Land Records and President of the Dakshina Bhiksha Committee which had the custody of the bulk of His Holiness' property during His lif[e]-time.

4. Mr. Hari Sitaram Dixit, Solicitor and at one time an additional member of the Bombay Legislative Council.

5. Mr. Moreshwar Wishwanath Pradhan, B.A. LL.B., Pleader, High Court, a well-known devotee of His Holiness.

6. Mr. Sakharam Hari Jog, retired Sub-Engineer.

7. Mr. Purushottam Sakharam Bhate, retired mamlatdar.

8. Mr. Shankarao Raghunath Deshpande, who was for several years Honorary Magistrate Sangamner.

9. Mr. Lakshman Balwant Pethkar, B.A. LL.B., High Court Pleader, who is a devotee of His Holiness and who has under His Holiness' orders been the Editor and General Manager of the Monthly religious Magazine called the Sainath Prabha or Dharma Rahasya.

10. Mr. Ganesh Damodar Kelkar a great devotee of His Holiness who has settled down in Shirdi and who is the Secretary of the said Daxina Bhiksha Committee.

11. Dr. Chidambaram Pillay retired veterinary inspector central provinces and a member of the Shirdi Sanitary Committee.

12. Mr. Tatya bin Ganpati Patil Kote, Chairman Shirdi Sanitary Committee.

13. Ramchandra bin Dada Kote, member Shirdi Sanitary Committee.

14. Mr. Mahadeorao Balvant Deshpande, member Shirdi Sanitary Committee.

15. Fatia Baba Pai [Pir] Mohomed, a leading member of the Mohomedan Community and payer of income tax at Shirdi.

Mr. HARI SITARAM DIKSHIT

(Sd.) C.A. BEYTS
District Magistrate, Ahmednagar

Sainath Prabha Kiran 11, 1918: 16–18

The Sansthan working committee decided to establish a marble statue of Sai Baba in Shri Sai Samadhi Mandir on 31st October 1920. However, this was constrained by lack of funds. A big photo of Sai Baba was placed behind the Samadhi, located in the centre on a silver platform. Prayers were offered and it was wrapped around with pitambar (yellow cloth), gandh (tika) and garland was put on it (*Shri Sai Leela* 1933: 2).

In the year 1954, Sai Baba's marble statue was installed in the Samadhi Mandir, that is Buti wada, after performing the prescribed rituals.

*****

Notes

1. *Shri Sai Leela* (1983: 25).
2. "Upasani, the great devotee, went to the banks of the holy Bhagirathi, along with Jog and performed the H[h]om-havan. And after feeding the Brahmins, giving anna-daan to the poor and after offering dakshina, as prescribed by the Shastras, they then returned." (Kher 2014: 731–732).

2

Shri Sai Baba Comes to Shirdi

This chapter discusses the possible time of the arrival of Shri Sai Baba in Shirdi, the period of his stay at Shirdi and his age at the time of his demise.

There exist various theories regarding the advent of the young fakir in Shirdi during the second half of the nineteenth century who later became well-known as Shri Sai Baba of Shirdi. Initially, he was known only to the people of Shirdi and a few surrounding villages. Gradually, the young Sai acquired prominence and became famous. In those days, village Shirdi was located in the Central Provinces, which included the present-day states of Maharashtra, Madhya Pradesh and Chhattisgarh. At present, village Shirdi is located in the Rahata taluka of district Ahmednagar in the state of Maharashtra, India.

Today, Sai Baba is not only a household name in India but is also known globally. We can find his pictures and photographs affixed in the front and rear windows of any number of vehicles moving on the streets of Maharashtra and even in metropolises like Delhi and Ahmedabad. His pictures and calendars can be found in shops and public places in urban, semi-urban and rural areas. It is difficult to make a complete list of the number of temples where he is worshipped in India and abroad. He is addressed reverentially by his devotees as Shree Sai Baba, Shirdi Sayin Baba, Shree Sainath, Sairam, Sadguru Sai or Sai Samartha and a few others with different epithets attached to his name (*Sainath Prabha* 1916).[1]

Shri Sai Baba's Arrival and Stay in Shirdi: A Brief Review of Different Times Mentioned in the Literature

Shri Sai Satcharita, which is regarded as the most authentic and most widely-read anthology on Sai Baba, mentions that Sai Baba made his first advent in Shirdi in the year 1854, stayed there for three years and then left. He returned in 1858 with the marriage party of Chand Bhai Patil and settled in Shirdi till his Mahasamadhi on 15th October 1918.

> Baba first came to Shirdi when he was a young lad of sixteen and stayed there for three years. Then, all of a sudden, He disappeared for some time. After some time, He reappeared in the Nizam state, near Aurangabad and again came to Shirdi, with the marriage-party of Chand Patil, when He was about twenty years old. Thence, He stayed in Shirdi for an unbroken period of sixty years, after which Baba took His Mahasamadhi in the year 1918. From this, we can say that the year of Baba's birth is approximately 1838 AD.
>
> Gunaji 2002: 58[2]

However, this statement of Govind Raghunath Dabholkar, alias Hemadpant, about the visits of Sai Baba to Shirdi, although popular, has not been accepted by many of the writers. There is difference of opinion on whether he came to Shirdi once and for all and settled down or he moved out for some time and settled down permanently on return. The number of days he stayed in Shirdi during the first visit and the time lag between the two visits is also not clear. Such confusion is due to scant availability of primary evidence pertaining to the arrival and departure of Sai Baba to and from Shirdi. Further, over a period of time, various concepts based on hearsay have crept into his hagiography.

Besides Dabholkar, some other writers like Ganpatrao Dattatreya Sahasrabuddhe alias Dasganu, B.V. Narasimha Swami, M.V. Kamath, V.B. Kher, Lt. Col. M.B. Nimbalkar,

Acharya Ekkirala Bhardwaja and others have tried to collect data from possible sources on this issue and have arrived at some probable theories.

> His wife's newphew [nephew] was to be married to a bride at Shirdi, and so in 1872, he came in the evening or night with a huge procession and Sai Baba accompanied him on that occasion from Dhupkheda to Shirdi. . . . So his final residence was Shirdi from about 1872 till the end of his life in 1918.
>
> Swami 1994a: 10

Another author mentions,

> He first came to Shirdi between 1868 to 1872 AD with Chand Patil of Dhupkheda, who came for the marriage of his sister with Hamid, the son of Aminbhai of Shirdi. . . . After a few days, Sai Baba and Chand Patil left for Aurangabad. Two months later, however, Sai Baba returned alone to Shirdi.
>
> Kamath and Kher 1995: 6

These writers have spent a lot of effort in the collection, collation and dissemination of the data and stories about Sai Baba in the form of books and articles.

Regarding the date of arrival of Sai Baba in Shirdi, B.V. Narasimha Swami, who visited Shirdi during the period 1935–36, are relevant.[3] He states that Sai Baba arrived in Shirdi in the year 1872.

The views of Narasimha Swami are of immense value for the researchers and writers for he had collected a lot of data and information on Sai Baba through detailed research, which included statements of the living disciples who had the opportunity of interacting with Sai Baba directly.

Shri Sai Satcharita mentions that Sai Baba returned to Shirdi in 1858 with the marriage party of Chand Bhai Patil of village Dhupkheda. The difference between 1858 as mentioned by Dabholkar and 1872 as mentioned by Narasimha Swami is fourteen years. Further, whether the marriage was conducted in Shirdi in 1858 or any other year is also not clear.

According to Dabholkar's statement, if Sai Baba came to Shirdi in 1854 at the age of sixteen and stayed there for three years before going away, it would mean that he left Shirdi at the age of nineteen in 1857 (date and month unknown) and returned with the marriage entourage of Chand Bhai Patil at the age of twenty in 1858. This leads to the conclusion that he was absent from Shirdi only for a few months.

Calculating backwards, Dabholkar presumed that since Sai Baba breathed his last on 15th October 1918 (Shaka year 1840), at the age of eighty, he would have been born in the year 1838 because in 1854 he came to Shirdi as a sixteen-year-old lad. Further, since Sai Baba returned and finally settled in Shirdi in the year 1858 and breathed his last in the year 1918, he had lived there for sixty years.

If we are to go by Narasimha Swami's view that Sai Baba was sixteen years old in 1872, then it would indicate that Sai Baba was born in AD 1856. This contradicts Dabholkar's statement that Sai Baba was born in 1838. According to Dabholkar, the number of years that Sai Baba stayed in Shirdi was sixty years but according to Narasimha Swami, it was forty-six years (1918 minus 1872). However, the date of Mahasamadhi of Sai Baba is universally accepted to be 15th October 1918 (*Sainath Prabha* 1918: 16–17).[4]

Ramgir Bua in his interview with Narasimha Swami states:

He was then accompanied by one Patel of Dhupkheda, who came to settle the marriage of a girl with Hamid, the son of Aminbhai of Shirdi. Baba appeared to be 25 or 30 years old, at that time. He stayed then as a guest of Aminbhai. In a very short time, (i.e.) after a few days, Baba and Patel went

back. Two months latter [later], he returned to Shirdi. He
returned alone and since that date made Shirdi his permanent
residence. . . . Baba was living under that tree for 4 to 5
years . . . he moved to the Mosque. . . . Baba lived about
50 years here (i.e.) after his arrival.

Swami 2006: 278–279

Another author has supported this view that Sai Baba
came to Shirdi when he was about thirty.

We cannot be sure which year Baba arrived in Shirdi, nor
how old he was, though it is usually estimated as being
between 1864 and 1872, at an age of about thirty.

Williams 2004: 9

If Sai Baba was 25 or 30 in the year 1872, then by
the time of his Mahasamadhi he would have been 71 or
76 years old respectively. This adds to further confusion.
Narasimha Swami's account indicates that Sai Baba would
have been born between the years AD 1842 and 1847. It
also says that after the marriage ceremony was over, Sai
Baba and Patil went back to Dhupkheda village. After
two months Sai Baba returned to Shirdi and lived there
permanently. This is the second visit story of Sai Baba to
Shirdi presented by Narasimha Swami. The first story is
the one stated by Dabholkar in *Shri Sai Satcharita*.

While many writers agree with Dabholkar, they are still
extremely cautious in fixing the dates of Sai Baba's advent
in Shirdi. Some fix the age of Sai Baba at the time of his
arrival in Shirdi at sixteen and some state it as thirty.[5]

Thus, there is a variance of fourteen years between the
different estimates of Sai Baba's age when he first arrived
in Shirdi (from sixteen to thirty years) and a difference
of eighteen years between the estimates of the year of his
arrival (1854–1872).

Given the differences of opinion among the authors regarding Sai Baba's year of birth, year of his advent and the years of his stay at Shirdi village, we need to address the following issues for clarity:

- The year in which Sai Baba came to Shirdi for the first time and finally settled down, if the one-time-visit theory is taken into consideration. Accordingly, the duration of his stay in Shirdi during his first visit also needs to be examined.

- The year in which he left Shirdi and the period of time (year and month) after which he returned to settle down finally, if the second-visit theory is taken into consideration.

- The age of the young fakir on his first arrival and the second arrival in Shirdi.

- The age of Sai Baba at the time of his Mahasamadhi.

- The total duration of his stay in Shirdi after he finally settled there, till his Mahasamadhi.

Shri Sai Baba's Arrival and Stay in Shirdi: An Analysis of Available Evidence

The different scenarios in this regard are as follows:

1. *Shri Sai Satcharita* mentions that:

> At noon, Bayjabai, mother of Tatya Kote Patil used to enter the forest carrying a basket of bhakris on her head. Wandering mile after mile, in search of the fakir in thick shrubs and bushes in the forest she would trace the mad fakir and fall at his feet. She fed a frugal meal of dry or curried vegetables and bhakri.
>
> *Dabholkar* 1930: 148, self-translated

The words "Bayjabai, mother of Tatya Kote Patil" can indicate that at the time when Bayjabai used to carry a basket of food articles on her head for feeding the young Sai Baba, Tatya would have been born.

The question is, how old was Tatya when his mother met Sai Baba for the first time?

Tatya was close to Sai Baba and addressed him as "Mama" which means maternal uncle.[6] Such was their mutual affection that there is no parallel to the feeling of affinity between them. He used to sleep in Dwarkamayi Masjid with Sai Baba for fourteen years and was virtually reared by him.[7] Oh, how wonderful were those days!

3. Further, a statement of Tatya Kote Patil in *Sainath Prabha* magazine (in the presence of four members of the Dakshina Bhiksha Sanstha) puts more light on this.

Tatya's statement that "Shri Samarth Sai Baba has reared me from my very birth" shows that Sai Baba would have come to Shirdi when he was born. He mentioned:

> I am a resident of Shirdi. Shri Samarth Sai Baba has reared me from my very birth. My parents are also at his constant service. We considered him as our father and family Deity and continue to do so till date. Approx. 12 years ago, Shri Sai never used to take any dakshina from anyone. He used to take Bhiksha from some particular houses of the village for his living. During my childhood, my parents used to fulfil some of his needs. As I grew up, after my father's demise, I am fulfilling some of his needs.

> *Sainath Prabha* Kiran 1 1916: 43–47, self-translated

4. The local school, where Tatya was studying, mentions his age. This date of birth of Tatya is important as there is a link between the date of arrival of Sai Baba in Shirdi and the birth of Tatya.

The school that Tatya attended maintained a Students Admission Register. It contains information regarding the name, caste, age at the time of admission, date of admission, year/month, date and year of leaving the school, fee detail and reasons for quitting the school for all students.

This school used to be inspected by the Sub-Inspector of schools, some of whom were Britishers. The details of Tatya Kote Patil as mentioned in the Students Admission Register are given in table 2.1.

Table 2.1: Students Admission Register of the school at Shirdi, in which Tatya Kote Patil studied

S. No.	Name of the child	Caste	Age	Admission date	Year/ Month	Date & Year of leaving the School	Whether father/ guardian was depositing fees	Reasons for quitting the school/ Behaviour of the child/ Child leaving in which class/Remarks
53.	Tatya Vald Ganpati Kote Patil	Kunabi	15	02.07.1887 (3rd standard)			Missing	Missing	Missing

In serial no. 53 of the original Students Admission Register, there is a mention about Tatya son of Ganpati Kote Patil being admitted in third standard in the year 1887 at the age of fifteen years. The date 2nd July 1887 is shown as the date of admission of Tatya and not his date of birth (photograph 2.1).

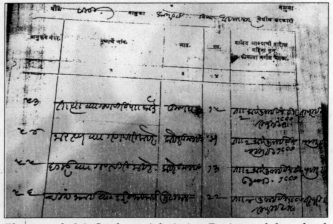

Photograph 2.1: Students Admission Register of the school (serial no. 53 mentioning the name of Tatya son of Ganpati Kote Patil)

This leads to the possible conclusion that Tatya Kote Patil was born in the year 1872.[8]

5. Statement of Hari Sitaram Dixit alias Kakasaheb Dixit in *Shri Sai Leela Maasik Pustak* (monthly magazine):

The introduction to *Shri Sai Satcharita* published in the book *Shri Sai Leela* is written by *"Babanche ek Lekru"*, in Marathi, which in English means "a child of Baba". This Lekru (child) of Sai Baba is none other than Hari Sitaram Dixit. Dixit writes that "Shri Sainath Maharaj first came to Shirdi approximately fifty years ago" (*Shri Sai Leela* Issue 1 1923: 1, self-translated). This indicates that Sai Baba came to Shirdi in around 1873 (photograph 2.2).

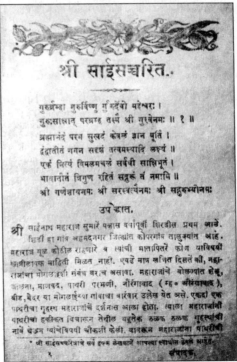

Photograph 2.2: *Shri Sai Leela* Issue 1, 1923 (Shaka 1845): Statement of Hari Sitaram Dixit in the chapter *"Shri Sai Satcharita – Introduction"* in the book *Shri Sai Leela*

6. The intelligence/enquiry reports of the Criminal Intelligence Department of the Colonial Government in India:

The weekly report of the Director of Criminal Intelligence, Calcutta, dated 17th January 1911 can be seen in photograph 2.3.

Weekly report of the Director of Criminal Intelligence, dated Calcutta, the 17th January 1911.

9. *Ahmednagar.* — Shortly after his return from England G. S. Khaparde of Amraoti went with his son Balkrishna to visit a *fakir*, said to be a Mahomedan, at Shirdi in the Kopargaon Taluka of this district; he arrived on 5th December 1910, and bowed himself before him thrice a day for a week. The *fakir* is an old man of about 70 who came to Shirdi some 30 or 35 years ago and put up in the village mosque where he has resided since. For a long time he was regarded as an ordinary *fakir,* but in the last 15 years he has acquired a great reputation for sanctity, and goes by the name of Sai Baba. He is

---

Photograph 2.3: Weekly report of the Director of Criminal Intelligence, Calcutta, dated 17th January 1911

According to the report dated 17th January 1911, Sai Baba was about 70 years old in January 1911, which means he was born in and around the year 1841. The report also says that he came to Shirdi around 30–35 years earlier. Deducting 30–35 years from January 1911, we can assume that Sai Baba arrived in Shirdi somewhere between the years 1876 and 1881.

The police sleuths, often put down the age of a person on the basis of hearsay if proof of the date of birth is not available. This report does not agree with the assertion of Dabholkar that Sai Baba came to Shirdi in 1854. It also does not mention about his second visit to Shirdi in 1858 and his age being sixteen at the time of his first visit. According to the report, Sai Baba's age was around 35–40 when he first came to Shirdi.

7. Maharashtra State Gazetteers Report

Gazetteer notifications (1976) of the Government of Maharashtra (photographs 2.4 and 2.5) state the following:

a. The year 1872 as the arrival of Sai Baba in Shirdi.

b. The marriage party arrived in the year 1872.

c. Sai Baba was sixteen years of age on his arrival in Shirdi in 1872. Nowhere is it mentioned that he had come for the first time, left for some time, revisited Shirdi and finally settled there.

He is said to have come to Shirdi in the year 1872 along with a marriage party when he was a handsome lad of sixteen years only.

Maharashtra State Gazetteers,
Ahmadnagar District 1976: 925

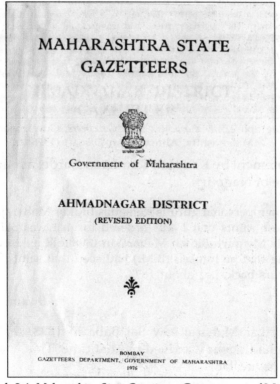

Photograph 2.4: *Maharashtra State Gazetteers,* Government of Maharashtra, Ahmadnagar District (Revised Edition) (1976) – Cover page

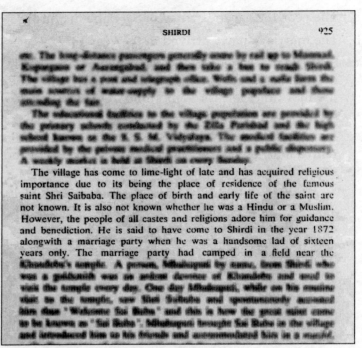

SHIRDI   925

The village has come to lime-light of late and has acquired religious importance due to its being the place of residence of the famous saint Shri Saibaba. The place of birth and early life of the saint are not known. It is also not known whether he was a Hindu or a Muslim. However, the people of all castes and religions adore him for guidance and benediction. He is said to have come to Shirdi in the year 1872 alongwith a marriage party when he was a handsome lad of sixteen years only. The marriage party had camped in a field near the

Photograph 2.5: *Maharashtra State Gazetteers*, Government of Maharashtra, Ahmadnagar District (1976)

7. A statement by Kasinath Kanderao Garde, a retired Sub-Judge of Nagpur:

My own personal guru is Ramadas Bidkar Maharaj. . . . One of these saints that I was ordered to visit was Sai Baba of Shirdi. My guru Bidkar Maharaj in 1898 told me to visit him, saying that he himself (B.M.) had seen that saint (Sai Baba) 25 years back, i.e., about 1873.

Swami 2006: 212

If Bidkar Maharaj saw Sai Baba in 1873, that means Sai Baba had already arrived by that time. That could even be 1872 or earlier.

8. According to one theory, Sai Baba went from Shirdi to Aurangabad, but returned.[9]

The period of absence varies from two months to seven months and more. On return he settled permanently in Shirdi.

9. Entry regarding the death of Shri Sai Baba of Shirdi in the Birth and Death Register of the Kopargaon Tehsil Office

In serial no. 120 of this register there is an entry about the death of Shri Sadguru Sai Baba on 15th October 1918 written in Modi/Marathi language, mentioning that Sai Maharaj passed away of fever and asthma at the age of 86. However, the age of 86 does not seem to be correct in view of predominant evidence stated in this book (photograph 2.6).

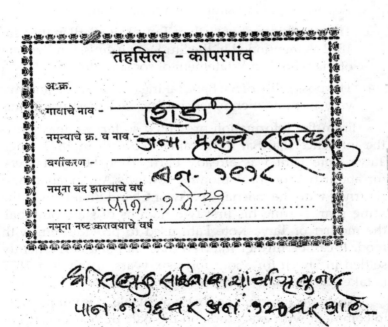

Photograph 2.6: Birth-Death Register of Tehsil Kopargaon

Shri Sai Baba's Arrival and Stay in Shirdi: Inferences Regarding timelines Based on Available Evidence

Given the information collected from various sources including authentic official documents, the following inferences can be drawn:

1. The possibility of the years 1872 or 1873, more correctly 1872, being the year of arrival of Sai Baba in Shirdi as stated by (i) Narasimha Swami (1872), (ii) Kakasaheb Dixit's statement in *Shri Sai Leela* (1873), (iii) Maharashtra State Gazetteers Report 1976 (1872), (iv) Alison Williams (between 1864–1872), and (v) Bidkar Maharaj's statement (1873).

2. The possibility of the arrival of the marriage entourage (of Chand Bhai Patil) in Shirdi along with Sai Baba in 1872 as recorded by Maharashtra State Gazetteers Report 1976, Narasimha Swami and some others.

3. The possible year of birth of Tatya Kote Patil in the year 1872 as mentioned in the Students Admission Register of the school and statement of some writers.

4. The possibility of Sai Baba taking care of Tatya since his very birth as mentioned in *Sainath Prabha* magazine.

From the information presented so far, we may draw the inference that Sai Baba came to Shirdi in 1872 when Tatya Kote Patil was already born. Then he went away for about two or three months, towards Aurangabad and returned with the marriage party of Chand Bhai Patil in the same year. During his first two months of stay, Bayjabai, the mother of Tatya Kote Patil used to provide him with food. It can be further inferred that Sai Baba permanently settled in Shirdi for about forty-six years, if the year 1872 is taken as the date of his arrival.

Given the information that is available, it is not possible to comment with exactitude on the date or year of birth of Sai Baba or on the age at which he reached Shirdi. However, the confirmed date is the date of his Mahasamadhi, which is 15th October 1918.

*****

Notes

1. *Sainath Prabha* (1916: v, 4, 9, 12, 13, 15, 22, 25). Shree Sai Baba, Sai Samarth (capable amongst all beings), Shree Sai Nath, Shree Sai Maharaj, Shree Sai Saguna Daya Murti (an idol of mercy having divine attributes), Shree Sai Parabrahma (Supreme Creator), Shree Sai Taponidhi (a great ascetic), Shree Sai Munivarya (greatest of all saints), Shree Sai Prabhu (Lord).

2. Dabholkar (1930: 172–173, self-translated).

3. Swami 2006: Preface.

4. *Sainath Prabha* (Kiran 11 1918): Obituary letter to Collector and District Magistrate, Ahmednagar from Hari Sitaram Dixit and endorsed by Rao Bahadur Hari Vinayak Sathe. "On behalf of and as directed by the Shri Sainath Sansthan Committee, I beg to inform you with deep regret His Holiness Shri Sai Baba of Shirdi breathed His last on Tuesday the 15th instant" (*Sainath Prabha* Kiran 11, 1918: 16–17; Ibid Kiran 10, 1918: Shri Samarth Sai Maharaj Prasann).

5. Sai Baba's date of arrival in Shirdi – a few excerpts from the literature:

   a. "Sai Baba first arrived in Shirdi in the year 1868 or so with the marriage party of one Chand Patil of Dhupkheda . . . after a few days, Sai Baba and Chand Patil went back. Two months later, Baba returned to Shirdi alone and passed the next fifty years there until his Mahasamadhi in 1918." He has also mentioned that "when Sai Baba came to Shirdi, he was a young man of thirty years" (Kher 2008: xii).

   b. "Sai Baba's 'second' arrival at Shirdi is indicated by Dabholkar (Hemadpant) as having occurred in 1858, and dated by Narasimha Swami to 1872. The difference is substantial enough to merit due caution" (Shepherd 2015: 7).

   c. "Sai Baba was about sixteen years old on his first visit to Shirdi . . . after being seen there briefly, he disappeared for a period, which ranged from two months to seven years. . . . On his second visit, variously dated 1858 or

1872, he remained in Shirdi permanently . . . and he
resided there until his death 50 or 60 years later in 1918"
(Warren 2011: 38).

d. "He had first appeared in the . . . little town of Shirdi as a
lad of sixteen in 1872 as wandering fakirs do" (Osborne
1972: 11).

6. Swami (1994a: 207).
7. Dabholkar (1930: 149 translated).
8. Aher (2017: 185).
9. Sai Baba and Chand Patil left for Aurangabad and after
two months, Sai Baba would have returned alone to Shirdi
(Rigopoulos 1993: 46). "He said he went to Aurangabad in one
of the wanderings" (Khaparde undated: 38).

3

The Governor's Lance

An explanation of Shri Sai Baba's statement to a devotee (Laxmibai Khaparde) about saving her husband (Ganesh Shrikrishna Khaparde) from the wrath of the British Government.

Introduction

This chapter tries to discover the meaning and check the veracity of a cryptic and mystical remark that Sai Baba is reported to have made to Laxmibai Khaparde, wife of Ganesh Shrikrishna Khaparde alias Dadasaheb Khaparde, on 29th December 1911.[1] This was Dadasaheb Khaparde's second visit to Shirdi and he was accompanied by his wife, Laxmibai, and his son Balkrishna Khaparde alias Babasaheb Khaparde. He stayed at Shirdi from 6th December 1911 to 15th March 1912. In one of his diaries, Dadasaheb Khaparde has noted down the key points of his conversation with Sai Baba in a laconic fashion (photograph 3.1).

Photograph 3.1: G.S. Khaparde with his family

He sent me a word this afternoon that I have to stay here another two months. He confirmed the message in the afternoon and then said that his "Udi" had great spiritual properties. He told my wife that the Governor came with a lance, that Sayin Maharaj had a tussle eith [with] him, and drove him out and that he finally conciliated the Governor. The language is highly figurative and therefore difficult to interpret.

Khaparde undated: 37

Sai Baba was well-known for uttering cryptic sentences, at times with the use of symbols, metaphors and parables, when communicating with his devotees. Numerous anecdotes reflecting this style of speech can be found in *Shri Sai Satcharita* and in the vast literature available on Sai Baba.

Some of his statements quoted in *Shri Sai Satcharita*, the most authenticate anthology on Sai Baba, indicate the manner in which Sai Baba used to communicate about incidents occurring in the past, present or future, to a particular individual while sitting amid a group of devotees, in a figurative and cryptic language[2] which only the targeted person could decipher. In certain cases, the purport of the words or sentences made by him would reveal its significance at an appropriate time in the future. This has been one of the most intriguing facets of Sai Baba's personality.

Sai Baba never made tall claims of his mystical or spiritual powers, even though certain events that used to take place around him bordered on miracles.[3] He uttered various gnostic words and statements when in a mood of spiritual ecstasy. This is indicative of his intense divine longing. Yet, characteristically, most of the time he described himself as a slave of Allah or God, who was inspired to undertake what the Allah commanded him. The frequent use of the word "Allah" reflects his unorthodox Sufi style of communication. Some of his utterings, as recorded in the diary of Abdul, are replete with the use of such a style.

Many anecdotes in *Shri Sai Satcharita* are indicative of such a style in which Sai Baba communicated with his devotees, even on matters of vital importance in a cryptic manner. For example, Sai Baba made a promise to Kakasaheb Dixit that "He will take him in air coach (viman)", (i.e., secure him a happy death) (Gunaji 2002: 255). The mystical word "air coach" or "viman" was not understood by anyone present there, including Kakasaheb Dixit. The word "viman" stands for an aeroplane or any flying vehicle. Most of the devotees believe that this assurance given by Sai Baba to Kakasaheb Dixit came true even after his Mahasamadhi. Dixit was travelling in a train with Hemadpant and was deeply engrossed in talking about Sai Baba, when he suddenly "threw his neck on Hemadpant's shoulder, and breathed his last with no trace of pain or uneasiness" (Ibid.). Given the Hindu religious belief of pushpak viman, it can also be interpreted that Sai Baba had secured sadgati or moksha or salvation for Kakasaheb Dixit.

The foregoing narrative shows that even if Sai Baba uttered something which appeared to be unclear, mystical or trivial, it never went in vain. The purport of Sai Baba's statement made to Laxmibai Khaparde, as recorded in the diary of Khaparde, needs to be understood in this light.

The Khaparde Diaries

Ganesh Shrikrishna Khaparde was a famous lawyer of Amravati, Maharashtra which was located in the Central Provinces during the British rule and which is currently located in the state of Maharashtra. He was the Chairman of the Reception Committee of the Indian National Congress (INC) held in Amravati in 1897,[5] before it split into moderates and extremists in 1907. Later, he joined the extremist group of the INC headed by Lokmanya Bal Gangadhar Tilak.[6] Following the inauguration of Montagen–Chelmsford Reforms, he was selected as a member of the Imperial Legislative Council. He also became a member of the Central Legislative Assembly between 1920 and 1925. Born on 27th August 1854, he has left behind a vast treasure of information in the forty-six diaries that he wrote during his lifespan. These consist of one pocket-dairy of 1879 and forty-five other diaries which were written during the period from 1894 to 1938.[7] These are mostly written in English. He passed away at the age of 84 years on 1st July 1938.[8]

Shri Saibaba Sansthan Trust, Shirdi, has published a book captioned *Shirdi Diary of The Hon'ble Mr. G. S. Khaparde* (photograph 3.2). The book has 141 pages. The first 107 pages comprise entries made during the visits of Khaparde to Shirdi. The book also includes two appendices written by V.B. Kher. Appendix-I is titled "More about 'Shirdi Diary' of Dadasaheb Khaparde" (pages 108 to 125) and Appendix-II is titled "Shirdi Diary and Mrs. Laxmibai Ganesh Khaparde" (pages 126 to 141).

However, we are concerned with his diary-notes written during his five visits to Shirdi and notes from his meetings with Sai Baba from 5th December 1910 to 12th December 1910 (first visit), 6th December 1911 to 15th March 1912 (second visit), 29th December 1915 to 31st December 1915 (third visit), 19th May 1917 (fourth visit) in the company of Lokmanya Bal Gangadhar Tilak and March 1918 (fifth visit, for unspecified number of days).[9]

During his second visit to Sai Baba from December 1911 to March 1912, his wife Laxmibai Khaparde and son Balkrishna Khaparde accompanied him and they spent a long time at Shirdi.

SHIRDI DIARY
OF
The Hon'ble Mr. G.S. Khaparde

Photograph 3.2: G.S. Khaparde's diary

Khaparde's diary note dated 29th December 1911 mentions about the statement that Shri Sai Baba made to his wife about his (Sai Baba's) tussle with the Governor and conciliation with the Governor in order to save Khaparde. Khaparde admits his incapability to understand the purport of the highly cryptic and figurative language used by Sai Baba.

Babasaheb Khaparde, in the biography of his father Ganesh Shrikrishna Khaparde (Dadasaheb Khaparde), interprets the words "lance of the Governor" as "arrest warrants", "trishul" as "Baba's divine power" and "Udi" as "the grace of Sai Baba" (Khaparde undated: 118; Khaparde 1962: 423).

However, the author has stated candidly at the outset that:

> The book is not a biography but edited material gathered from Dadasaheb Khaparde's daily diaries and letters for the purpose of the biography.

> Khaparde 1962: 3, self-translated

An analysis of these notes in the diaries leads to the following conclusions: Dadasaheb Khaparde, admittedly, could not decipher the meaning of the words spoken by Sai Baba. The use of metaphorical, symbolic and figurative language is a method adopted by many saints, particularly, in the Sufi tradition, which Sai Baba frequently adopted. Sadgurus and saints are believed not to speak untruths, even though, at times, the meaning of their figurative language may not be clear.

Shri Sai Baba's Tussle with the Governor to Save Khaparde: Fiction or Reality?

The first thing to understand is whether what Sai Baba said was anecdotal or fictional.

The words indicate that Sai Baba was referring to a certain situation of the past in which the Governor was adversely disposed towards Khaparde due to some reason and was trying to harm him. Whether Sai Baba was referring to an issue of the future, present or past could have been clarified at that time if Khaparde or his wife had sought a clarification from Sai Baba, which they did not.

After his second visit, Khaparde had three more chances to meet Sai Baba during his subsequent visits to Shirdi. Yet, he did not seek any clarification. Probably, he did not consider it important. It is interesting to note that even a brilliant lawyer like Khaparde, who had fought the sedition case against Lokmanya Bal Gangadhar Tilak in the Privy Council at London, could not understand the purport of Sai Baba's statement!

Sai Baba's saying that he "had a tussle with the Governor", obviously, implies that it was a matter of the past in which Sai Baba had seriously exerted himself in order to save Khaparde from the lance of the Governor, that is, he saved him from an adverse situation. The word "lance" was used symbolically and metaphorically and need not necessarily be interpreted as the Governor trying to kill Khaparde physically with a lance. The appropriate interpretation may be that the colonial British Government had hatched some sort of a conspiracy to cause serious trouble for Khaparde. Sai Baba could foresee it and was able to save him. We have to understand what type of trouble it was and what type of influence, spiritual or otherwise, Sai Baba would have exerted to save Khaparde as at that time, there was no apparent connection or communication between Khaparde and Sai Baba before they met physically for the first time.

After the division of the Indian National Congress into extremist and moderate groups in 1907, following the Partition of Bengal in 1905, Khaparde became a close associate of Tilak, the leader of the extremists group. Tilak was arrested on charges of sedition on 24th June 1908.[10] He was confined in Mandalay Jail, Rangoon, presently known as Yangon, the capital of Myanmar (erstwhile Burma). His trial began on 13th July 1908 and he was convicted and sentenced to six years imprisonment on 22nd July 1908. In order to fight the case in the Privy Council, Khaparde, as his lawyer, reached Dover on 31st August 1908 and proceeded to London.[11]

> Within a few days thereafter, i.e. on 15th August 1908, Dadasaheb sailed for England to prefer an appeal to the Privy Council against the judgement of the Bombay High Court convicting Lokmanya . . . Khaparde sailed for India via Rangoon on 15th September 1910 after a stay of over two years in England . . . Khaparde reached Rangoon on 16.10.1910 and met Tilak in Mandalay Jail on 22.10.1910. Having reached Calcutta on 27.10.1910, he returned home on 5.11.1910 after an absence of two-years, two months and twenty-two days.
>
> Khaparde undated: 116–117

Photograph 3.3: Bipin Chandra Pal, Lokmanya Bal Gangadhar Tilak and G.S. Khaparde in front of the Parliament in London to appear before the Privy Council in the sedition case against Tilak

On return from London and Yangon, Khaparde paid his first visit to Shirdi on 5th December 1910, followed by a second visit (6th December 1911 to 15th March, 1912). At that time, he did not have any idea about any conspiracy being hatched against him by the colonial government of British India, although he may have had lurking doubts. Nevertheless, the words "Governor came with a lance, that Sayin Maharaj had a tussle with him" (Khaparde undated: 37) were sufficient indicators given by Sai Baba about an adverse and dangerous situation against Khaparde that had already taken place. The words "he finally conciliated the Governor" indicated that the issue was reconciled before Khaparde met Sai Baba. Some authors have also mentioned this issue.[12] They have just quoted the diary note without adding any comment.

Khaparde had failed in his mission in London and returned to India disappointed. On arrival in India, he found that he was being monitored by the Intelligence Department, at his home, office or wherever he went. These may be the reasons of his visit to Sai Baba.

Basically, a person of worldly wisdom, Khaparde seemed to foster high political and material ambitions. His professional trajectory shows his exponential rise from the status of a small-town lawyer to a member of the Imperial Legislative Council and also a member of the Central Legislative Assembly.

When he met Sai Baba in Shirdi, the latter had also pointed out his weakness for material pursuits. Khaparde was not the only beneficiary of such type of kindness of Sai Baba to protect someone without an obvious prior connection. The anecdote relating to Upasani Maharaj, who used to be protected by Sai Baba even before he met Sai Baba in Shirdi, exemplifies such kindness.[13]

In the realm of religion and spiritualism based on faith, devotees are prone to believe the statements of gurus or saints like Sai Baba. On the other hand, persons who don't follow such a path are likely to raise questions in this regard. For instance, they could suggest that Sai Baba may have received the information regarding the danger lurking on Khaparde from one of his devotees, linked with the political or government circles, or could have heard a rumour. Khaparde visited Sai Baba because he was apprehensive about the diabolic intentions of the British Government, given the suspicious activities of the intelligence agents around him. In 1913, based on his diary entry dated 1st April 1913, his diaries got stolen which was another suspicious activity that happened.[14]

Shri Sai Baba's Tussle with the Governor to Save Khaparde: Analysis Based on Primary Evidence

How can we prove that Sai Baba had saved Khaparde from the wrath of the Governor? Rationally, proving such an action will require documentary and primary evidence like government files, reports, notes and similar confidential documents.

Fortunately, this researcher could locate a document which we will call the "Cleveland Report".

During the Queen's rule, the Home Department of India received political and criminal intelligence reports collected through the Directorate of Criminal Intelligence or C.I.D. (Criminal Intelligence Department) usually headed by a British officer belonging to the Indian Civil Service (I.C.S.). Such reports, categorized as A, B, C, and D, dealt with different issues of the government. For example, in the Cleveland Report, Political Report A mostly consisted of classified and important documents, Political Report B contained the weekly intelligence reports sent to the Headquarters of the Director of Criminal Intelligence located in Kolkata, consisting of the intelligence reports from the provinces, that is, Bombay, Bengal, Central Provinces, and so on. At the field level, such reports usually originated from plain-clothed police personnel. These reports were used by the British Government to control the insurgent Swadeshi movement and identify its leaders. The reports were used as inputs to create new policies and amend the existing ones to minimize and contain, overtly and subvertly, any type of insurgent activity by Indian nationalists and extremists.

Seditious activities of individuals, organizations and groups, as well as newspapers, journals and books were also reported to the Viceroy of India. Lord Curzon was the Governor-General and Viceroy of India from January 1899 to November 1905 and Lord Gilbert Elliot-Minto held the position between November 1905 and November 1910.

Shirdi village, located in the Central Provinces had a special system of administration whereas Bombay and Bengal had a different system.[15]

The Chief Commissioner of the Central Provinces was akin to the Governor of other provinces such as Bombay, so far as the administration of the Central Provinces was concerned. R.H. Craddock, then Chief Commissioner, sent a demi-official letter on 19th March 1909, to Sir Harold Stuart, then the Home Secretary, enclosing the Cleveland Report and recording his own remarks regarding the activities of the disloyal party in Nagpur (Annexure-2). He proposed the deportation of G.S. Khaparde and Balakrishna Shivram Munje under Regulation III of 1818 to St. Helena (a remote tropical island in South Atlantic Ocean which was a part of the British territory). This record is a "strictly confidential" record of 1909 of the Government of India, Home Department, and is categorized as "Political-deposit covered by the Proceedings of June, 1909, No. 3". This Cleveland Report deals with the political situation of India, particularly in Nagpur and Central Provinces, and brings out the role of G.S. Khaparde and B.S. Munje in insurgent activities following the division of the Indian National Congress in 1907. Both Khaparde and Munje were activists of the extremist group led by Lokmanya Bal Gangadhar Tilak.

Thus, the report shows that the Government had seriously started following the seditious activities of the disloyal party in Nagpur from July 1907, that is, even before the Indian National Congress was divided into moderate and extremist groups in December 1907 in the Surat Session of Congress.

> Lord Curzon decided upon the partition of Bengal into two or more manageable units, Western Bengal which included Bihar and Eastern Bengal with which Assam was linked. The partition aroused a great movement of Bengali patriotism and much agitation in which Hindus and Muslims both took part. This was the outstanding example of regional patriotism, but it was matched in other parts of India and notably in the Maratha region around Poona, where also the extremist found fertile soil for their revolutionary intrigues during the decade 1900–10.
>
> Newton 1947

The indictment of Khaparde recommended by R.H. Craddock was based on his (Khaparde's) speeches of 1905 (para-18), photographs, newspaper publications, intelligence collected through criminal intelligence agencies and also statements of witnesses and other relevant evidentiary documents. Comments were recorded on the file by R.H. Craddock, H.A. Damson and H.A. Stuart. The file was then sent to H.A. Damson, Member of the Council of the Governor-General and, finally, went for perusal of the Viceroy, Lord Minto, whose observation dated 23rd April 1909 reads:

> The papers are very interesting and should be circulated. It would be altogether inopportune to raise the question of deportation under present conditions.

This entire file was processed during Khaparde's stay in London. As we saw earlier, Khaparde had left India on 15th August 1908 and came back to India (Calcutta) on 27th

October 1910, after a period of two years, two months and thirteen days.[16] None of the notes in the diary written by Khaparde during his stay in London indicate that he was aware of any move by the British Government to indict and deport him to St. Helena after his proposed arrest in the Port of Addam. The decision of Lord Minto against his deportation was taken in May 1909. Till then, Khaparde had no connection with Sai Baba.

Khaparde's diary mentions that he was in the blacklist of the Government. Commenting on *Shirdi Diary of Dadasaheb Khaparde*, Kher comments that Dadasaheb paid a visit to Shirdi for a week, within a month of his return from England. By that time the political situation had deteriorated and the Government was increasing its actions of repression to suppress the national movement. The arrest of Bipin Chandra Pal on 7th October 1911 for sedition also indicated this. Since Khaparde had been agitating for the release of Lokmanya Tilak, he was on the blacklist of the Government and his arrest was imminent.[17] Sensing this, Khaparde's eldest son visited Shimla to meet the Chief Officer from the Detective Department to gather first-hand information about the Government's intention.[18]

The diary-note of Khaparde about Sai Baba's statement can be divided into two parts:

Part I: *He sent me a word this afternoon that I have to stay here another two months. He confirmed the message in the afternoon and then said that his "Udi" had great spiritual properties.*

As discussed earlier, even if the issue of his deportation was closed by the Viceroy against the recommendations of R.H. Craddock, the threat of arrest and deportation was kept alive. It is possible that Sai Baba, through his divine power of clairvoyance, had foreseen the impending danger on Khaparde. Hence, he went on deferring the departure of Khaparde from Shirdi many times, extending it up to two months, till 15th March 1912, when he allowed him to go home.

Part II: *He told my wife that the Governor came with a lance, that Sayin Maharaj had a tussle eith [with] him, and drove him out and that he finally conciliated the Governor. The language is highly figurative and therefore difficult to interpret.*

The first part explains the circumstances under which Sai Baba extended Khaparde's stay in Shirdi by two months while the second part deals with Governor who had come with a lance and was finally conciliated by Sai Baba. Thus, Part I indicates a current situation and Part II indicates a past problem which was averted due to the intervention of Sai Baba.

From the examination of all the information we have received so far, it seems that the problem of the past could possibly be the proposal of deportation of Khaparde as recommended by Craddock, the Chief Commissioner, having the powers of a Governor of the Central Provinces and hence the de-facto Governor. It also means that Sai Baba, through his spiritual powers, had influenced the minds of the British Government officials at various levels not to deport Khaparde to St. Helena.

Many such references regarding the powers of Sai Baba to know the past and future of his devotees can be found in *Shri Sai Satcharita*.[19] Some Indian and Western writers have also mentioned about this power of clairvoyance that Sai Baba often displayed.[20]

Neither in the Marathi book *Shri Dadasaheb Khaparde Yanche Charitra* written by G.S. Khaparde's son, Balakrishna Khaparde, nor in any other book, is there any mention about Cleveland Report and the communication of Craddock, the Cheif Commissioner of Central Provinces and Berar. Cleveland Report is, perhaps, the first report dealing with insurgent and seditious activities of the nationalistic Indians in the Central Provinces. If Babasaheb Khaparde had any knowledge about this report, he would have certainly mentioned it in his book. If G.S. Khaparde had an idea about it, he would have mentioned it in his diary as well.

Craddock would have destroyed Khaparde's life and career if his recommendation of deportation of Khaparde to St. Helena had been accepted, for the Chief Commissioner of the Central Provinces exercised power akin to the Governor of other provinces and could have been addressed as Governor. Metaphorically speaking, he had raised his sharpened lance (i.e., his report) to kill Khaparde's career. The file containing the report passed through the hands of several other officials of the Government and the Members of the Council of the Viceroy till the recommendations were finally dropped by the Viceroy, Lord Minto. This is what is meant when Khaparde wrote in his diary that Sai Baba had a tussle with the Governor and he was saved. The conciliation was not to deport him to St. Helena and to control him through other weapons of the political armoury available with the British Government.

*****

Notes
1. Khaparde (undated: 37).
2. Gunaji (2002: 84).
3. Ibid: 177–178.
4. Khaparde (undated: Preface); Khaparde (1962: 7).
5. Khaparde (1962: 26 translated).
6. Khaparde (undated: Preface).
7. Ibid: 111; Khaparde (1962: 1).
8. Khaparde (1962: 3).
9. Khaparde (undated: 113).
10. Khaparde (1962: 327); Khaparde (undated: 116).
11. Khaparde (undated: 116).
12. Shepherd (2015: 261); Kher (2008: 124); Swami (1994: 281).
13. Swami (2005: 27).
14. Khaparde (1962) mentions that nine diaries of Dadasaheb Khaparde were missing. The diaries used to be kept in a wooden box in the hall where people used to come and go. Therefore, the loss of diaries from such a place is very

surprising. Dadasaheb Khaparde in his diary note on 1st April 1913 mentions that "Missing dairies could nowhere be found. This is very mysterious and I do not know what to think of it. . . . They have wonderfully enough disappeared. Dorle had made a list of missing dairies" (Khaparde 1962: 452).

15. The *Imperial Gazetteer of India*, Issue. IV, Administrative (1909), in chapter II titled Administrative Divisions states that, the provinces directly under the administrative control of the British Government were of two types, viz., Regulation Provinces and non-Regulation provinces. In both kinds of provinces the questions of policy or of special importance were submitted for the orders of the Governor-General of India. The provinces of Bombay, Madras, Bengal and Agra (a part of United Provinces) were called "regulation provinces" while Central Provinces along with Punjab, Burma, Oudh and Assam were non-regulation provinces. The provinces of Bombay and Madras were administered by Governors while Bengal, United Province, Eastern Bengal, Assam, Punjab and Burma were administered by Lieutenant Governors. The Central Provinces, were however, administered by the Chief Commissioner.

16. Khaparde (undated: 116–117).

17. Ibid: 117.

18. He stayed with Dada Saheb's friend Ajijuddin, a senior officer in the Criminal Intelligence Department for three days. On return to Amravati, he performed "*Arimaran naavanche rudra devateche ikvis divas anushthan kele*". Details of this puja are covered in the monthly magazine *Sahaydri* under an article "Mantra Shakti" (Khaparde 1962: 422, 423).

19. Gunaji (2002: 192–195).

20. Some statements are given here:
   "Sai Baba loved his devotees and anticipated their wishes and movements. There are innumerable instances where Sai Baba clairvoyantly knew ahead of time when something would occur" (Warren 2011: 68).

"Some people he would ask for Rs. 5, some for Rs. 25, and some others for Rs. 250. Almost every one that he asked would pay. Baba knew the minds and state of the purse of all and could get exactly what he wanted" (Rigopoulos 1993: 144).

"Others seemed to take pains and make efforts to read the contents of people's minds and tell them their past history, but with Sai Baba no effort was needed. He was always in the all-knowing state" (Osborne 1972: 31).

4

The Govindas at Dwarkamayi

This chapter highlights the role of the detectives at Dwarkamayi in Shirdi during Shri Sai Baba's time.

We saw Sayin Maharaj go out, and saw him later at the Musjid. He told a long story which in substance was that an old Patil used to visit him, that four and afterwards as many as twelve Govindas (Detectives) used to watch him, that the old man and the Govindas had hard words and once had a serious scuffle. Sayin Sahib favoured the old man, visited him in this field and on one occasion hit the Govindas when they attacked him. At last the old man was removed to a large town for being dealt with, that Sayin Sahib intervened and got him released.

Khaparde undated: 105

Sai Baba, the famous saint of Shirdi, lived through a tumultuous period of Indian history after the first Indian War of Independence of 1857 and during the First World War. He entered Mahasamadhi on 15th October 1918.

During the period of his stay in Shirdi, India witnessed a sea change. The rule of the Mughal emperors had ended with the deportation of Bahadur Shah Zafar by the British to Rangoon in Burma, followed by his death on 7th November 1862, at the age of 87.[1] Without the royal patronage, the sustenance of the Muslim culture and Urdu language became difficult and its dominance dwindled. With the establishment of British colonial hegemony over the Indian territory, after the War of Independence in 1857, English as a language, Christianity as a religion and Western culture started gaining a strong foot-hold on the Indian soil. It was a period of churning in the socio-cultural and political history of India. Mohan Das Karamchand Gandhi who was destined to become the "Father" of the Indian nation was still far away.

The Indian National Congress (INC) was formed in the year 1885. It became the fulcrum of the Indian Independence Movement under Gandhi's leadership in later years. The spirit of nationalism was awakened. At this critical juncture, Lord Curzon's reactionary policy of stringent opposition to Indian nationalism led to the enactment of the Official Secrets Act of 1904 and the Indian Universities Act of 1904.

This accentuated the disgruntlement of the Indians. The Partition of Bengal Act of 1905 segmented East and West Bengal on the basis of religion and divided Hindus and Muslims, which led to a division in the Indian National Congress between the extremist and the moderate groups in 1907. While for the moderates British rule was not all evil for India, the extremists wanted to attain complete independence from the autocratic British rule. They viewed armed struggle and the use of violence as appropriate methods to achieve Swaraj.[2]

Lord Curzon tried to strengthen the police organization in India through police reforms. A Criminal Intelligence Department (C.I.D.) was established as a central unit along with administrative units at district levels to keep an eye on the insurgent and seditious activities of individuals, groups, organizations and Indian media demanding and fighting for Swaraj.

A police station had many villages under its jurisdiction and was responsible for dealing with incidents and recording information on a number of issues like law-and-order, crimes, criminals, festivals, ingress and egress of people to-and-from the villages, epidemics, births and deaths, execution of court documents like summons and warrants, and so on. The Shirdi village was covered by the Rahata Police Station, presently located in district Ahmednagar of Maharashtra State.

Sai Baba's name and fame gradually grew among the people of Shirdi and the neighbouring villages during the last two decades of the nineteenth century and first two decades of the twentieth century when there was a lot of political and social flux. Insurgency and revolutionary groups created a lot of problems for many people in the political and social spheres and also in the offices of the Indians working under the Britishers. After 1908, a large number of people from all sections of society, both urban and rural, started visiting Shirdi, enamoured by the tales of Sai Baba's kindness, generosity and powers of miracles (Swami 1994b: 13).[3] He was known for treating everyone with kindness, engaging in philosophical, religious and ethical conversations and providing guidance on how to act. He also discussed mundane matters and helped in solving their problems. He shared food, chillum and joked with them at his abode, the Dwarkamayi. He played the dual role of a guru and a protector to all his devotees, without any consideration of caste, religion, creed, gender, position or temporal status. Sai Baba mostly spoke in rustic Marathi language in his daily conversation with devotees, which was highly cryptic and figurative. Both rural folks and the educated elite from large towns and cities in the Central Provinces (now Maharashtra) addressed him with epithets like Guru, Fakir and Sadguru.

One of the most important visitors to Sai Baba in Shirdi was Ganesh Shrikrishna Khaparde, an eminent lawyer from Amravati. He was a close associate of Lokmanya Bal Gangadhar Tilak, who led the extremist wing of the INC for achieving Swaraj (photograph 4.1).

Later, Khaparde became a Member of the Imperial Legislative Council.[4] Between 1920 and 1925, he was a member of the Central Legislative Assembly.

Photograph 4.1: Lokmanya Bal Gangadhar Tilak sitting with G.S. Khaparde

He wrote forty-six diaries – one pocket diary of 1879 and forty-five full-sized diaries written between 1894 and 1938.[5] For our purpose, the diaries of 1910, 1911, 1912, 1915 and 1917 are important as these were written during his five visits to Shirdi and contain a vast trove of information about Sai Baba and the events at Shirdi.

Surveillance of Shri Sai Baba and His visitors by the British Intelligence Agencies

While going through Khaparde's diary entry of 13th March 1912, which has been quoted at the beginning of this chapter, the word "Govindas" drew my attention. This word is mentioned thrice in this note.[6] When mentioning "Govindas" for the first time, Khaparde followed it with the word "Detectives" within brackets. He did not reproduce the entire conversation with Sai Baba verbatim in his diary but only wrote short notes of what Sai Baba had said. There is no indication to suggest that Sai Baba had explained to Khaparde what the word "Govindas" stood for. Perhaps the context in which Sai Baba talked about the issue indicated to Khaparde that the Govindas were British detectives. Khaparde had close professional connection with the police, judiciary, courts and the government officials working there. Hence, it would be naive to assume that he did not know that C.I.D. was keeping a watch on Sai Baba.

The diary entries under reference narrate about an old Patil who was watched by four to twelve detectives (Govindas) during his visit to Sai Baba. Words were exchanged between them, followed by an altercation. Subsequently, the Govindas attacked the old man, removed him to a large town in order to deal with him, where Sai Baba intervened and got the old man released.[7]

Khaparde has not clarified if what Sai Baba said was intended to be factual or another of his cryptic or mystical statements. Khaparde's diary clearly suggests that the C.I.D. was observing Sai Baba's activities and those of his visitors. At times, they took stringent measures including physical assault, removal and detention of the suspects. Since Sai Baba met many people at Dwarkamayi on a daily basis, it stands to reason that many C.I.D. agents would be in Dwarkamayi, keeping a watch on everyone.

Let us review the activities of the Govindas in Dwarkamayi and the real purpose of their visit.

To this purpose, five questions have to be answered: a) Did the C.I.D. or the police department keep a watch on Sai Baba's activities during the period of his stay in Shirdi, either in uniform or in plain clothes? If so, what were the reasons. b) Were any such report(s) of the sleuths sent to the higher echelons of the Government? c) What were the views of the Government about Sai Baba? d) If these three answers are in affirmation then what action, if any, was contemplated or taken by the Government? e) Did Sai Baba, directly or indirectly, ever participate in discussions or render advice on political or seditious activities?

The books written on Sai Baba so far do not throw much light on these issues. Therefore, collection of information from hitherto unknown sources that throw light on the subject becomes necessary.

By the beginning of the twentieth century, Sai Baba had become a famous spiritual personality whom people held with great reverence. Following the well-established guru-shishya (teacher-student) tradition of India, they also gave him a lot of money as dakshina.

> Every evening, he disposed off the entire collection retaining nothing and saving nothing. Of these some were given fixed amounts i.e., regular daily payments e.g. to Bade Baba of Rs. 30/-, to Tatya Patel Rs. 9 or Rs. 10 to Lakshmi, the supplier of daily bread, Rs. 4, etc.

> Swami 2004: 367

Devotees offered dakshina totalling ₹400–500 to Sai Baba daily.[8] Since Sai Baba gave away at the end of the day whatever he received in charity during the day to people like Bade Baba, Tatya Kote Patil, Laxmibai, Ramchandra

Dada Patil Kote and others, the Income Tax Department collected tax from Bade Baba and Tatya Kote Patil and not from Sai Baba as he was not found to be the beneficiary of such collections.[9] This indicates the watchfulness of the government about the activities going around Sai Baba. A large number of government officials visited him, including magistrates, revenue and police officers. So did judges, lawyers, businessmen, political activists, academicians, farmers, labourers, musical and acrobatic entertainers, wrestlers, kirtankars, pandits, priests, fakirs, devotees and common folk – all were readily taken under his benevolent fold. This may have been another reason to keep him under intelligence coverage.

At that time, political reporting in C.I.D. was of four types: Political - A, Political - B, Political - C and Political - D. This system of reporting continued till 1923, when the single filing system was introduced by the Imperial Government in India. Here we are primarily concerned with the Political reports A and B. Political - A consisted mostly of classified and important documents, whereas Political - B consisted of the weekly reports sent by the Director of Criminal Intelligence (D.C.I.) to the Home Department. These were printed reports, with the front page mentioning the date of the report, the number of the proceedings and the number of pages contained in the report. These rare documents provide valuable primary evidence while assessing the activities of intelligence agencies around Sai Baba and also their views about him. The three reports of the D.C.I., collected from the National Archives of India are the weekly reports of the D.C.I. on the political situation during January 1911, July 1912 and August 1912. These are discussed in the following section.

Selected Weekly Criminal Intelligence Reports and Other Documents: An Analysis

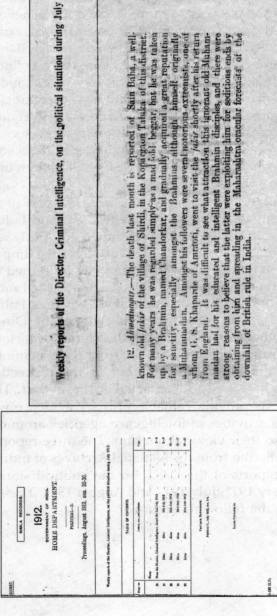

Weekly reports of the Director, Criminal Intelligence, on the political situation during July

12. *Ahmednagar.*—The death last month is reported of Sain Baba, a well-known old *fakir* of the village of Shirdi, in the Kopargaon Taluka of this district. For many years he was regarded simply as a mad *fakir*, but he was taken up by a Brahmin, named Chandorkar, and gradually acquired a great reputation for sanctity, especially amongst the Brahmins, although himself originally a Muhammadan. Amongst his followers were several notorious extremists, one of whom, G. S. Khaparde of Amraoti, went to visit the *fakir* shortly after his return from England. It was difficult to see what attraction this ignorant old Muhammadan had for his educated and intelligent Brahmin disciples, and there were strong reasons to believe that the latter were exploiting him for seditious ends by obtaining from him and spreading in the Maharashtra oracular forecasts of the downfall of British rule in India.

Photograph 4.3: Weekly reports of the Director, Criminal Intelligence, on the political situation during July 1912: Proceedings August 1912, nos. 26–30

Photograph 4.2: Cover page of weekly reports of the Director, Criminal Intelligence, on the political situation during July 1912: Proceedings August 1912, nos. 26–30

BOMBAY.

11. *Ahmednagar.*—A patel constable on his rounds in the Newasa *taluka* of this district came across in one of the villages a Maratha with an earthen bowl in his hand which he tried to conceal. The constable called up one or two people as witnesses, and seized the bowl in their presence. It contains *[illegible]* ... first, apparently, copied at different times from different works. In one ... it is stated that Marathi-knowing people should consider themselves all of one caste, and should tramp on the enemies of their religion and not hesitate to kill them. In another is an exhortation to sow corn from the people who kill ... bland. ... is stated at an appeal to right in united array to clear the ... up into the breast of the enemy, and so forth. The bowl was obtained by ... Maratha about three years ago from G. V. Gore, a schoolmaster, who ... is in connection with the Ahmednagar conspiracy. Further enquiries are ... ing the people concerned: the seditious literatures has a seditious nature in the village.

12. The report of the death of Sain Baba (*vide* paragraph 12 of *[illegible]* Weekly Report, dated the 16th July 1912), the old Musalman *fakir* who numbers among his disciples many Brahmins and not a few leading extremists, appears to be incorrect; the man who died was a Musalman priest of the same neighbourhood named Saiba. Those disciples of Sain Baba, who live at his place and manage his affairs, are said to be of very low class, using him merely as a means of making money on which they live in idleness and vice.

Photograph 4.5: Weekly reports of the Director, Criminal Intelligence, on the political situation during August 1912: Proceedings September 1912, nos. 21–24

Photograph 4.4: Cover page of the weekly reports of the Director, Criminal Intelligence, on the political situation during August 1912: Proceedings September 1912, nos. 21–24

Weekly Intelligence Reports: July and August 1912

Report No. 12 dated 17th July 1912 gives an account about the death of a person known as Sain Baba. A subsequent intelligence report dated August 1912 clarifies that the report regarding the death in Kopargaon did not refer to Shri Sai Baba of Shirdi but to another Muslim priest by the name of Saiba who lived in Kopargaon.

During the initial years, Sai Baba of Shirdi was regarded as a mad, old fakir because of the unpredictable behaviour of a mendicant that he manifested. This indicates that Sai Baba rose to prominence for his spirituality much later. Some devotees like G.G. Narke, Shama and even Mhalsapati considered Sai Baba to be senile at a point of time.

The report says that his rise to prominence as a spiritual leader was because of a Brahmin called Chandorkar. This was Narayan Govind Chandorkar alias Nanasaheb Chandorkar, Secretary to Deputy Collector, Ahmednagar who superannuated as Deputy Collector, Thane.[10] Chandorkar first came to Sai Baba in 1892[11] when Sai Baba was not very widely known. He was one of the earliest of Sai Baba's influential devotees, who was instrumental in spreading his name. Chandorkar was the inspiration behind the visits of Hari Sitaram Dixit, Dasganu, Balkrishna Vishwanath alias Balasaheb Deo, M.W. Pradhan and many more, to Sai Baba at Shirdi.[12]

Sai Baba's social acceptability and credibility increased due to the support of these educated and prominent Brahmins. Some of them like Kakasaheb Dixit, Nanasaheb Chandorkar and Balasaheb Bhate, dedicated their lives to spreading Sai Baba's name and fame, far and wide.

From among Sai Baba's devotees who had political connections, Khaparde belonged to the extremist group of the INC. Hari Sitaram Dixit alias Kakasaheb Dixit, a famous solicitor and an active member of INC,[13] was elected as a member of the Bombay Legislative Council from 1901.[14]

He belonged to the moderate group of INC. However, except Khaparde and Tilak, there is no mention about other extremists visiting Sai Baba, although it is said that a few of them had visited him.

According to his diary, Khaparde visited Shirdi shortly after his return from England on 5th December 1910.[15] Later, he took Lokmanya Bal Gangadhar Tilak, the leader of his extremist faction of the INC, to Shirdi for the darshan of Sai Baba on 19th May 1917.[16]

> After Tilak had departed from the mosque, the District Collector of Ahmednagar arranged for a CID officer to infiltrate Shirdi. This measure was for the purpose of monitoring activities of the faqir. . . . Some believe that the contact between Tilak and Baba was politically significant, inferring that the latter's covert message to the former amounted to: Indian Independence would only be gained through non-violent action, not by violent measures.
>
> Shepherd 2017: 128

This indicates that the C.I.D. was active in Shirdi even at the time when Tilak visited in 1917 and thereafter.

The intelligence report obviously shows that the sleuths of C.I.D. could not fathom the reason and depth of the attachment of such educated people with Sai Baba. With their preconceived notions and biases, the intelligence personnel were unable to understand the relationship between the highly educated Brahmins and the apparently ignorant Sai Baba. They failed to grasp the tenets of the guru-shishya tradition in the Indian socio-religious context, where a religious or spiritual guru is held in the highest social esteem even if he lacks formal education. As per the occidental concept, a guru stands for a teacher or at best, a mentor. In India, the guru is compared with God and is also believed to possess divine powers.

Having failed to appreciate this connection between Sai Baba and the Brahmins, the detectives resorted to speculation. This is a classic case of people preferring any explanation to no explanation of some things they do not understand.

Hence, it was natural for the sleuths to presume that the Indian extremists would be taking the help of astrologers and soothsayers to get them to relay forecasts about the expected end of the British rule in India in order to inspire the general public against the British.

Weekly Intelligence Report Dated 17th January 1911

The Weekly Intelligence Report dated 17th January 1911, S. No. 9, of the Director of Criminal Intelligence shows that Khaparde consulted an astrologer in Amravati (photograph 4.6) before his trip to England on 15th August 1908.

Weekly report of the Director of Criminal Intelligence, dated Calcutta, the 17th January 1911.

9. *Ahmednagar.* – Shortly after his return from England G. S. Khaparde of Amraoti went with his son Balkrishna to visit a *fakir*, said to be a Mahomedan, at Shirdi in the Kopargaon Taluka of this district; he arrived on 5th December 1910, and bowed himself before him thrice a day for a week. The *fakir* is an old man of about 70 who came to Shirdi some 30 or 35 years ago and put up in the village mosque where he has resided since. For a long time he was regarded as an ordinary *fakir*, but in the last 15 years he has acquired a great reputation for sanctity, and goes by the name of Sai Baba. He is described as a *Sadhu*, is said by some to be an *Avatar*, has little following among Mahomedans, practices none of the devotions, etc., of their faith, but is supported by many more or less distinguished Brahmans such as the Honourable Mr. Hari Sitaram Dikshit, Mr. Chandorkar (Deputy Collector and formerly Mamlatdar of Kopargaon) and many others. One Mamlatdar named Bhate, formerly in Khandesh, was so devoted to Sai Baba that he resigned his post and now lives at Shirdi as a kind of devotee.

So far as can be ascertained it appears that the *fakir* is approached on purely religious grounds, and it is not easy to account for Khaparde's visit, but the following explanation is suggested. It was reported in August last that before Khaparde left for England a secret meeting was held at his house at Amraoti at which astrologers of repute were requested to forecast the future of Maharashtra. The astrologers prophesied that by 1916 the present agitation would assume a tangible shape, and would go on increasing till 1920 by which time there would be actual recourse to arms, and by 1925 the British would have to leave the country. The forte of the Sai Baba of Shirdi is apparently to foretell the future, and Khaparde may have visited him in connection with this, possibly as a believer, but more probably, appreciating the effect of such prophecies on the minds of the people, in order to inspire the oracle.

Photograph 4.6: Weekly reports of the Director, Criminal Intelligence, Calcutta, dated 17th January 1911

This intelligence report is about the secret activities of Khaparde trying to find out about the end of the colonial rule in India which was a serious matter.

It was an accepted fact in the public domain that Khaparde was a political leader and Sai Baba was a spiritual personality of a very high order. Yet, someone may speculate that Sai Baba might have rendered advice to Khaparde on political issues. However, there is no evidence to suggest that Sai Baba encouraged Astrology or inspired his devotees to indulge in any sort of political activity or speculation.[17]

One example of Sai Baba's disdain for Astrology can be seen in the story of Raghunath and Savitribai Tendulkar's son. On hearing that her son, Babu Tendulkar, felt dejected because astrologers had predicted that the stars were unfavourable that year and so he should appear for the medical entrance examination next year, Sai Baba told Savitribai to tell her son to "throw aside horoscopes and predictions of astrologers and palmists and go on with his studies" and that he was "sure to pass this year."[18]

Nevertheless, the sleuths would have presumed that people approaching a religious and spiritual guru like Sai Baba would request for predictions and oracles on political matters, particularly about their freedom from the British rule. More so, because Sai Baba was famous for knowing the past and the future of people visiting him. Sai Baba, at times, would speak about details about the past, present and future of a person approaching him even without being asked.[19]

This report refers to Khaparde's first visit to Shirdi with his eldest son Balkrishna, from 5th December to 12th December 1910. This is mentioned in Khaparde's diary. Upon returning from England, Khaparde reached Calcutta via Rangoon on 27th October 1910.[20] He went to Bombay and then travelled to Shirdi by train.

As mentioned earlier, the report also describes Sai Baba as 70 years old, that he came to Shirdi some 30 or 35 years earlier and describes him as a Mohammadan, who had settled down in a mosque known as Dwarkamayi. From this, we can try to calculate the time his arrival in Shirdi, but given the discussion in chapter 2, this may not be the correct information. Further, this statement divides Sai Baba's life in Shirdi into two segments, before and after 1895. It says that Sai Baba has been called a Sadhu by most people and as an Avatar by some like Swami Sharananad. He was supported by more or less distinguished Brahmins like Honourable Hari Sitaram Dixit, Nanasaheb Chandorkar and Balasaheb Bhate. It is known that Bade Baba, Abdul Baba, Rohilla, Abdul Rahim, Abdullah Jan, Imam Bhai Chote Khan, Haaji Siddique Falke and others were well-connected with Sai Baba at Shirdi. Thus, it would be unfair to say that Sai Baba only had a "little following" among Muslims. Among them, Abdul stayed with Sai Baba for his whole life. After Sai Baba's Mahasamadhi, he served the Samadhi of Sai Baba. Further, many Sufi saints, dervishes and fakirs visited Sai Baba on their journeys. It is also incorrect to presume that Sai Baba did not practise any Muslim rites. He practised a few on certain occasions.[21]

The report also makes a mention about the prominent Brahmins who served Sai Baba namely Hari Sitaram Dixit, Gopalrao Mukund Buti and Balasaheb Bhate.[22]

Except the conjectures of the C.I.D. personnel, there is no evidence that Sai Baba ever made any political predictions. He neither advised any of his devotees on matters of politics nor encouraged any sort of political activism or prophecies. Had it been so, the intelligence report would have indicated it and some sort of action against Sai Baba would have been initiated by the government.[23]

Khaparde's diary also highlights the active role played by one detective in disguise during his visit to Sai Baba. In his Shirdi diary entry of 29th December 1911, there is a mention of one Mr. Natekar, also called Hamsa and

Swami. Khaparde learnt that Hamsa was a C.I.D. detective planted by the government in their household and that he had followed Dadasaheb to Shirdi to gather information about his activities there. Similarly, the diary note of 27th December 1911 states that detectives were stationed near Sai Baba.[24]

This gives a clear idea that detectives used to be posted near Sai Baba in Dwarkamayi to listen to the questions asked by the devotees, including those who had a political background and Sai Baba's answers. Had any dialogue on political issues taken place between Sai Baba and any of his devotees, it would certainly have been reported to the government.[25]

In this context, the statement of a police officer, who was deployed to collect intelligence at Shirdi, becomes useful to understand if Sai Baba said anything political to his devotees who were inclined towards politics.

Chakranarayan was the police Fouzdar of Kopargaon at the time of Sai Baba's Mahasamadhi. Shirdi is situated at a distance of about 11 miles from Kopargaon (*Sainath Prabha Kiran 1*, 1916: Approaches). In the British times, the Fouzdar used to be in-charge of a police station and was required to gather all types of criminal and political intelligence about individuals, groups and organizations, including insurgent activities, against the British government. Since Chakranarayan was a Christian who was more trustworthy to the ruling dispensation, it is possible that he was assigned to keep a watch on Sai Baba for various purposes, including the levy of income tax on the donations that Sai Baba received daily. Chakranarayan was interviewed by B.V. Narasimha Swami in 1936, eighteen years after the Mahasamadhi of Sai Baba. At that time Chakranarayan was the Reader to Police Deputy Superintendent, Thane, Maharashtra.

I was Police Fouzdar at Kopergaon when Baba passed away (October 1918). I was not a believer in Baba. We were watching Baba through our men. Even though I watched him sceptically, the result was to create in me a high regard for him. First and foremost was the fact that he was not moved by women or wealth. Many women would come to him and place their heads on his feet and sit before him. But he was unmoved; he would not care to cast one glance of admiration or of lust at them. He was clearly and unmistakably unattached. About money also, we watched him. People voluntarily gave him money. If any did not give him money, Baba would not curse or hate or be displeased with him. The same held good about his begging for bread. He did not care for what he got. Whatever he got, he scattered with a liberal hand.

Swami 2006: 92

The statement of Chakranarayan also confirms that his police station kept a watchful eye on Sai Baba and his activities due to the visit of so many important personalities. Such police personnel are called "Govindas" in Khaparde's diary.[26] Calling a detective a "Govinda" is a typical example of Sai Baba's elusive manner of speech. Chakranarayan keenly observed Sai Baba's earnings and donations in order to assess his income tax liability. Since a part of his job was to gather intelligence about possibly seditious activities and Sai Baba frequently had political people as his visitors, Chakranarayan kept a close watch on the activities around him. In case he found any action of Sai Baba against the ruling regime, then he was duty-bound to report it to the higher authorities and action would have followed.

Role Played by Intelligence Agencies: Findings Based on Evidence

The weekly reports of the D.C.I. on the political situation during January 1911, July 1912, August 1912, September 1912, Cleveland Report of 1909, a few notes recorded in the diaries of G.S. Khaparde and the statement of Chakranarayan, Fouzdar of Kopargaon, together confirm that Sai Baba, and also the important devotees visiting him, used to be under surveillance by the police sleuths in plain clothes. The department also kept a watch on Khaparde whenever he used to meet Sai Baba inside Dwarkamayi.

Sai Baba must have spoken with thousands of people during his time. Yet, during the entire period of his stay at Shirdi for a few decades, he never made a single comment which can said to be political or seditious in nature. The reports of the D.C.I. and the statements of police officers like Chakranarayan show that Sai Baba was held as a pious man without any attachment towards women or money. Sai Baba was a Spiritual Master and a mentor to all devotees. His dwelling place, known as Dwarkamayi, was open to everyone all the time. He had no political interest or political views at all. The welfare of all living beings, and the evolution of the human souls to higher levels, was always his priority. He is a Saint par excellence who is believed to guide his devotees even after leaving his bodily form (Gunaji 2002).

*****

Notes

1. Nayar (2007).
2. According to one of the recommendations of the Police Commission of 1902, set up to reform the police in India, a Directorate of Criminal Intelligence (D.C.I.), headquartered at Calcutta, was created in India. Its district level units started functioning from 1906. Shirdi was covered by the D.C.I. functioning under the Collector/District Magistrate of Ahmednagar. This agency mostly consisted of police personnel in plain clothes who strategically donned different identities and attire like that of a sadhu or a beggar. Positioning themselves in different places to collect information, they sent weekly reports to the office of the D.C.I., headquartered at Calcutta, through the

office of the District Magistrate The D.C.I. collected, collated and disseminated these reports and sent them to the Government for review and necessary action. Some important reports could go up to the Governor-General or Viceroy located in Shimla during summer. For the village of Shirdi, the Fouzdar of Rahata police station was responsible to send reports to D.C.I. through the Collector/District Magistrate Ahmednagar.

3. The people who came to Shirdi after 1908 included Hari Sitaram Dixit (1909), Raghuvir Bhaskar Purandhare (1909), Ganesh Shrikrishna Khaparde (1910), Meghshyam Balwant Rege (1910) Govind Raghunath Dabholkar alias Hemadpant (1910), Ramchandra Atmaram Tarkhad, M.W. Pradhan. (1910), Balkrishna Vishwanath Deo (1910).

4. Swami (1994b: 277).

5. Khaparde (undated: 111–112), Khaparde (1962).

6. Khaparde (undated: 105).

7. Ibid.

8. *Shri Sai Leela* (Issue 4, 5 and 6, 1941: 16).

9. *Shri Sai Leela* (Issue 4, 5 and 6, 1942: 90).

10. *Shri Sai Leela* (Issue 7, 8 and 9, 1941: 50).

11. Ibid: 44.

12. "Chandorkar is a missionary of sorts, leading people to Shirdi and certainly was one of the most ardent propagators of Baba's fame in the region" (Rigopolous 1993: 123).

"Nanasaheb Chandorkar may be termed appropriately the first apostle or Saint Peter of Baba" (Swami 1994a: 149).

13. *Shri Sai Leela* Issue Nos 6–9 (1935: 22).

14. Swami (1994b: 144).

15. Khaparde (undated: 114).

16. Ibid: 124.

17. Gunaji (2002: 69).

18. Ibid: 155–156.

19. Ibid: 59–60.

20. Khaparde (undated: 116–117).

21. In this context, Swami (2006: 153) notes: "I do not think any other Mohammadan except myself was reading Koran or other

holy books sitting by Baba's side. Baba would occasionally go on speaking out sacred words. And I have noted them in this notebook."

On the same lines: "He did not wear the ochre robe of Hindu ascetics, and spoke the Muslim language of Deccani Urdu" (Shepherd 2017: 4). Or, "Baba knew Arabic and Urdu, and had taught the Koran to Abdul" (Swami 2004: 605).

22. Kaka Saheb Dixit built a wada (home) in Shirdi and spent his last years serving Baba. Gopalrao Buti also built the Buti wada, which has become the Samadhi temple of Sai Baba. Balasaheb Bhate was a Mamlatdar of Kopergaon Taluka, who decided to stay with Sai Baba for his whole life upon his first visit.

"Later, the thirteenth day (after Baba's niryan) was observed. Balasaheb (Bhate), a gem amongst the devotees, collected Brahmins from the village and began the funeral rites" (Kher 2013: 31).

"Afterwards, he came to Shirdi and Baba made him stay for six months on leave. He did not go to duty even after six months. His Superior (Personal Assistant to the Revenue Commissioner) came to Shirdi, and asked Bhate to rejoin duty. Bhate refused.... From that time, he left the post of Mamlatdar" (Rigopolous 1993: 109).

23. S. no 15, page 4, of Central Provinces – Weekly Report of the Director of Criminal Intelligence, 1911.

24. "Sai Baba remained aloof from the political scene and did not agitate in any way against the British rule" (Shepherd 2017: 128).

25. "I did not sleep well last night but got up early in the morning . . . the detectives here appeared to be more active than usual today. One stationed himself near Sayin Maharaj. Another followed me" (Khaparde, undated).

26. Ibid: 105.

5

Sathe Wada, Dixit Wada and Navalkar Wada

This chapter discusses the construction and the present status of the three wadas at Shirdi namely, Sathe wada, Dixit wada, Navalkar wada.

Introduction

The village of Shirdi is located in Kopargaon subdivision of district Ahmednagar, in the state of Maharashtra. It is situated on Maharashtra State Highway 10 (Ahmednagar–Malegaon). Over the last few decades it has become one of the famous spots of pilgrimage in India, as it houses the Samadhi of Shri Sai Baba, popularly known as Shirdi Sai Baba.

Sai Baba arrived in Shirdi during the second half of the nineteenth century. He lived there continuously till his Mahasamadhi on 15th October 1918. During the days of the British rule in India, Shirdi was a part of the Central Provinces. In those days, Shirdi used to be a small village consisting of about 1,500 persons.[1]

In those days, many villages had a place to rest for officials and other visitors coming to visit or stay in the village. The arrival and departure of such people often used to be recorded. According to the census report of 1976 in the *Maharashtra State Gazetteers*, Shirdi had a small built-up structure called the "Chawadi" for this purpose. Sai Baba started sleeping there on alternate nights from 1910 onwards.

After settling down at Shirdi, Sai Baba stayed in a dilapidated mosque called Dwarkamayi, a few steps away from the Chawadi. Apart from being a resthouse for lodging the visitors and travellers, the Chawadi was also a place for the villagers to get together for different purposes like holding discussions or majlis.

Usually such a resthouse had all its four sides open, although in certain other places it used to be a closed structure (photographs 5.1a and 5.1b).

Photograph 5.1a: Old Chawadi

Photograph 5.1b: Old Chawadi

Photograph 5.2: Chawadi now

The number of people visiting Sai Baba was increasing continuously. Important persons like judges, magistrates, revenue and police officials, lawyers, businessmen, academicians and many others started frequenting Shirdi to receive blessings and help from Sai Baba. Unfortunately, except the houses of relatives and friends, there was no place in Shirdi where the visitors could stay. The Chawadi was in a rather dilapidated and unliveable condition. Sai Baba understood the problem and therefore in 1906 he asked Rao Bahadur Hari Vinayak Sathe to build a wada. Accordingly, Sathe built the first wada in Shirdi. In building the wada, Sathe had the intention of creating a place for himself to stay as he frequented Shirdi, and also for the other visitors. Construction of this wada, which was known as "Sathe wada", was completed in 1908.[2]

It is interesting to note how three wadas were built in Shirdi during the first two decades of the twentieth century. This chapter deals with Sathe wada, Dixit wada and Navalkar wada (photograph 5.3). Navalkar wada was built within the premises of the Sathe wada.

Photograph 5.3: Artistic impression of the wadas (old) based on available references
Source – Created by Shirdi Sai Global Foundation (SSGF)

The fourth and the most important, Buti wada, known as the Samadhi Mandir, has been discussed separately in chapter 6.

These wadas played an important part during the days of Sai Baba as they housed a large number of devotees as well as the government officials visiting him from different parts of Maharashtra and elsewhere. Since there used to be a long line to meet Sai Baba at Dwarkamayi (photograph 5.4), these wadas scarcely remained empty. While some devotees stayed for short durations, others like Rao Bahadur Hari Vinayak Sathe, Kakasaheb Dixit, Govind Raghunath Dabholkar, Ganesh Shrikrishna Khaparde stayed for weeks and months.

For many who wanted to serve Sai Baba for long spells of time, the wada virtually became a home-away-from-home. People staying in the wadas performed many types of activities – religious, spiritual, social and, of course, personal. Various kinds of logistical support were available in the wadas. *Shri Sai Satcharita*, the most well-accepted anthology on Sai Baba, also provides some information about the three wadas.[3]

Photograph 5.4: Old Dwarkamayi

Sathe Wada

For a few years after Sai Baba arrived in Shirdi, the number of visitors was not much. By the year 1910, Shirdi was struggling to cope with the increasing influx of visitors, including a good number of urban dwellers from Mumbai, Ahmednagar, Nasik and other places. Children, differently abled, old, diseased and people with infirmities visited Sai Baba along with friends and companions. Following the prevailing norms of pilgrimage, people belonging to the same family or clan often accompanied them.

People travelled by trains, tongas (horse-pulled carts) or bullock-carts, while some came walking from long distances. Some had to travel for days to reach Shirdi. Hence, it was necessary to have night shelters and also other facilities at Shirdi to cater to the needs of the visitors. Pilgrimage to the temples or the ashrams of the gurus was not necessarily for only a few hours. At times, it stretched to weeks and months. Sai Baba also used to arrange the stay of some visitors in the houses of his local devotees.

Under these circumstances, the visit of Rao Bahadur H.V. Sathe to Sai Baba for the first time in April 1904[4] turned out to be a boon for the visitors, leading to the construction of a wada. Sathe was a person of considerable social standing. At the time of his first visit to Sai Baba, he was working under the colonial government as a Deputy Collector of Ahmednagar District. He learnt about Sai Baba from Mr. Bharva, the Mamlatdar of Kopargaon.[5]

Sai Baba fondly addressed Sathe as "Saheb".[6] Gradually, Sathe became a close devotee and a prominent worker serving Sai Baba. Being posted at Ahmednagar, he had the good fortune of being able to pay frequent visits to Shirdi and, therefore, had the pressing need of a resting place for himself. Therefore when Sai Baba suddenly asked Sathe to build a wada during their conversation, saying, "Pull down the village wall and build" (meaning to pull down a portion of the boundary wall of the village and build a wada using the boundary line as a wall), Sathe made up his mind to do so[7] (photograph 5.5).

Photograph 5.5: Old Sathe wada

Sathe bought this site, along with the neem (margosa) tree and the surrounding space. On a purnima (full moon) day in 1906,[8] when Ganesh Vishnu Behere and H.V. Sathe visited Shirdi, they found Sai Baba returning from Lendibagh (Ambekar 1997: 131–132). On seeing them, Sai Baba said, "Saheb, you have come at the right time. Today, we have to do the foundation work." Sathe, thinking that Sai Baba was asking for a small function to begin the construction of the Sathe wada, picked up a kudaal to start digging. Seeing this, Sai Baba said, "Why are you going there? What do we have to do in this? Villagers and workers will complete this work" (Ambekar 1997: 131–132). Then the digging of the land started.

There is an interesting anecdote regarding a long branch of the neem tree which hampered the progress of construction. No one dared to chop it off as "this tree had been sanctified by Baba's stay under it and also as Baba used to call it as his Gurusthan" (Swami 2006: 113). When they approached Sai Baba, he told the villagers, "Cut off however much is interfering with the construction. Even if it is our own foetus which is lying across the womb, we must cut it!" (Swami 2006: 113). Yet, no one dared. Eventually, Sai Baba came and cut off the branch himself. Thereafter, the wada was constructed.

> Sathe saheb, one of Baba's devotees, acquired the land all around it, along with the Samadhi and the neem tree and raised a building with four verandahs connected at the centre. This building, this very wada, was originally the common residence of the pilgrims, forever crowded with comings and goings of visitors. Sathe raised a bank around the neem tree and an upper floor running north-south. When the northern staircase was laid, he pointed out the cell. Under the staircase, facing south, is a beautiful niche. In front of it, facing north, the devotees sit on the bank.
>
> Kher 2013: 67–68

R.A. Tarkhad alias Babasaheb Tarkhad, visited Shirdi on 6th December 1910. He has described Sathe wada according to his own experience.[9]

> As entry is made from the front gate of wada, Mandali used to stay in front dalaan. On left dalaan, there was a hotel run by Late Balabhau Chandorkar, on right dalaan, facilities were made for families and here on a platform was a staying place for late Megha and his Puja arrangements. Sathe was occupying the first floor in the front and Noolkar with his Mandali taking room on the back side of the first floor. Noolkar would often come down and sit with Bhakta Mandalis.
>
> *Shri Sai Leela* Issue 1–2, 1930:1, self-translated

There were two gates in Sathe wada (north and south).[10] It is interesting to note that at the very place where the wada, including some portion of Buti wada (which was constructed later), was built, there was a flower-garden[11] grown by Sai for a period of three years (photograph 5.6).

Photograph 5.6: Artistic impression of the flower garden grown by Shri Sai Baba based on available references
Source – Created by SSGF

This Sathe wada is important for another reason, too. In the beginning, on the very spot, there was a beautiful flower-garden grown by Baba with his own hands.

Kher 2013: 70

Besides, Sathe wada was also important due to a few other reasons.[12] Sai Baba regarded the area under the neem tree as his Guru's seat.

"This is my Guru's seat," said he, "and my most sacred legacy. Listen to me this once and preserve it as it is." So said Baba, said the listeners who were present.

Kher 2013: 67

This was in 1910, when there was only one place, viz., Sathe's wada, for lodging pilgrim devotees.

Gunaji 2002: 8

The list of persons who inhabited the wada, on a long or short stay, is too exhaustive to mention. The names of a few important persons are – Ganesh Shrikrishna Khaparde, Ganesh Damodar alias Dada Kelkar and Govind Raghunath Dabholkar.

Aarti of Sai Baba's picture was conducted regularly at the wada by different persons, individually and in groups. Sathe wada was also utilized as a place of religious and spiritual practices, including meditation and reading religious scriptures, as prescribed by Sai Baba to some of the devotees, from time to time.

Bapusaheb Jog read *Eknathi Bhagawat* and *Gyaneshwari* sitting in Sathe wada.[13] Regular reading and discussion sessions of different scriptures like Ramayan, *Eknathi Bhagawat* and *Yoga Vasistha* were held in the evenings. Bhajan singing sessions took place at night. Krishna Shastri Jogeshwar Bhishma mostly sang the bhajans.

Tatya Saheb Noolkar breathed his last in this wada.[14] Megha, who started the congregational worship of Sai Baba,[15] stayed at the wada for a long time, till his death.

Another prominent feature was the installation of the padukas of Sai Baba under the neem tree in 1912. Sagun Meru Naik, Govind Kamlakar Dixit and Bhai Krishnaji Alibagkar wanted to install padukas in the memory of Sai Baba's arrival at Shirdi and his stay under this neem tree. These padukas were sent by Ramrao Kothari and had beautiful motifs. The padukas were first kept in the Khandoba Mandir and Bhai Krishnaji asked for permission from Sai Baba to install these padukas. Sai Baba said that they should be installed on the purnima (fifteenth day) of Shravan. On that day at 11 a.m., G.K. Dixit brought them on his head from Khandoba's temple to the Dwarkamayi (Masjid) in procession. Sai Baba touched the padukas, thus consecrating them and said that these were the feet of the Lord and asked the people to install them, at the foot of the neem tree. As per Upasani Maharaj's advice, the padukas were installed on a raised marble pedestal with the front panel having the inscription of the fourth verse of Shri Sainath Mahima Stotram, written by Upasani Maharaj, signifying the importance of the neem tree. At the time of installation of the padukas, Upasani Maharaj, Balasaheb Bhate, Bapusaheb Jog, Dada Kelkar and others were present (*Shri Sai Leela* Issue 1, 1934: 24–26). A small Shiv Pindi and Nandi were also installed there.

Even after the departure of Sai Baba, this wada continued to be used by visitors. Swami Sharananand, a well-known devotee of Sai Baba, regularly stayed in this wada whenever he visited Shirdi, till his demise in 1982.[16] By that time, Sathe wada had been purchased by Ramkrishna Shrikrishna Navalkar and hence was renamed as Navalkar wada.

Dixit Wada

Dixit wada was built three years after the Sathe wada.[17] It was meant to provide spacious accommodation to the visiting devotees[18] as well as to Kakasaheb Dixit and his family members whenever they visited Shirdi.

Dixit wada reduced the pressure on Sathe wada which till then was the only wada for visitors. Many historic events that took place in the Dixit wada have been recorded in *Shri Sai Satcharita*. Therefore, it would be relevant to know a little about Kakasaheb Dixit, who built the wada (photographs 5.7 and 5.8).

Photograph 5.7: Old Dixit wada

Photograph 5.8: Artistic impression of the wadas (old) based on available references
Source – Created by SSGF

Mr. Hari Sitaram alias Kakasaheb Dixit was born in 1864 AD, in a Vadnagara Brahmin family, at Khandwa. . . . His primary and secondary education was done at Khandwa, Hinganghat and Nagpur. In the year 1878, at the age of fourteen, he passed matriculation with very good marks at Nagpur and he got two scholarships. He came to Bombay for higher education and studied P.E. in the Wilson College and then passed B.A from the Elphinstone College at the age of nineteen. He got Dheerajlal Mathuradas scholarship. After this he passed LL.B. and the exam of solicitor. Then served in the firm of the Govt. Solicitors, Little and Co. and then after sometime he started a solicitors' firm of his own . . . he built a bungalow in Lonavla where he used to stay in summers.

Shri Sai Leela 1926: 405–410, self-translated

Besides being a successful solicitor of Mumbai High Court, he was an active member of the Indian National Congress[19] and an elected member of the Bombay Legislative Council.[20]

Kakasaheb Dixit visited England in the year 1906.[21] During his stay in England, his leg got injured when boarding a train in London. He tried different methods of treatment, but could not be fully cured of his lameness.[22]

Kakasaheb Dixit first visited Shirdi on 2nd November 1909.[23] He was overwhelmed by the compassion and divine personality of Sai Baba, which changed his life forever. He prayed to Sai Baba to cure the lameness of his mind rather than that of his leg. Sai Baba used to address him fondly as "Kaka"[24] or "Langda Kaka".[25] He re-visited Shirdi in December 1909, having decided to render service to Sai Baba for all his life. He decided to sell about twenty-five shares of his company and build a shed with a corrugated roof. However, later he decided to build a wada instead, which could be used by the devotees visiting Shirdi.[26]

"The foundation of this building was laid on 10-12-1910" (Gunaji 2002: 22). Kakasaheb's elder brother Baiji (*Shri*

Sai Leela 1935: 44) from Nagpur was also there and both of them worked very hard for completing the wada. As a result, the wada was ready in only six months. On the day of Ramnavami of 1911, the griha pravesha (the ceremony of entering a newly built house, "house-warming") was performed with all the rituals (Kher 2013: 70).

The wada was considered to be spacious compared to those built in those times.[27] On the ground floor, rooms were built for the visiting devotees. An arrangement was made for their meals at the back of the wada. On the first floor, Kakasaheb placed a large, framed photo of Sai Baba, made by Shamrao Jaykar.[28]

> As to the house or wada built by me at Shirdi, I direct the hall on the ground floor and the two front rooms and the verandah in the front as also the two tin roof sheds at the back be reserved for devotees visiting the shrine of Shri Sai Baba and making a temporary stay at Shirdi. The central portion of the wada consisting of a quadrangle and western and eastern rooms and inside verandah as also the hall on the upper floor shall be at the sole disposal of my heirs. I however, wish that they should not be sold or let out.

> *Shri Sai Leela* Issue 11–12, 1931: 25–26

> Land is 6 Guntha in area and does not have any legal owner in the official records. Kakasaheb's elder brother, Rajaram alias Bhaiji was a contractor who prepared a draft outline for the wada. The raw material and the workers were sent to Shirdi.

> Aher 2017: 156, self-translated

There is a reference of a land purchased by Kakasaheb Dixit in 1910 in Shirdi from one mendicant (bhikshuk), Laxman Bhatt for ₹150. The bhikshuk wanted ₹200 for the land but Kaka insisted on paying only ₹150. There was a dispute over the cost. Then when Laxman Bhatt was passing

in front of the Masjid, Sai Baba called him and asked him
the reason for the dispute. After hearing the details, Sai
Baba mediated and told him to accept ₹175 and nothing
less than it. But Laxman did not share with Kaka what
Sai Baba said. Finally, the deal was settled for ₹150 and
the land registry documents were prepared accordingly.
However, on returning home, Laxman saw that the money
given to him was ₹175 and not ₹150.[29]

K.J. Bhishma wrote his famous book *Shri Sainath
Sagunopasana* (the aarti book) while staying in this wada.
Other devotees like Babasaheb Tarkhad, his family and
Jyotindra stayed there during their visits.

Sunder Rao Dinanath Navalkar, Deputy Secretary,
Shri Saibaba Sansthan Trust, Shirdi, vide his letter dated
3rd February 1932, published the will of H.S. Dixit.[30]
According to his will, the specified portions as mentioned
were given to the devotees and to his heirs. Later, his sons
donated their portion to the Sansthan and gave them the
permission to offer this as a place to stay in Shirdi to the
visiting devotees.[31]

Sai Baba used to encourage his devotees to read sacred
books like *Jnaneshwari* and *Bhagawat*. "Once Baba asked
Balasaheb Deo to sit in Dixit wada and read *Jnaneshwari*
daily and regularly" (Dabholkar 1930: 704, self-translated;
Dabholkar 1930: 707, self-translated). Shri Sai Baba had told
Hemadpant to be with Dixit. So Hemandpant stayed in
this wada whenever he visited Shirdi. "He told Annasaheb
Dabholkar 'Kaka Saheb is a good man. Be guided by what
he says.' . . . He told R.B. Purandhare to be with Kaka
Saheb and assist him" (Swami 1994b: 146). Even Shama,
who was a local resident and a close devotee of Shri Sai
Baba, stayed in the wada at times, and took care of it.[32]

In this wada, there was a small room upstairs which
was used by Kakasaheb for "Ekanta Dhyana". Sai Baba once
said, "Kaka, remain in your wada upstairs. Do not go here
or there. Do not come here, even to the Dwarakamayee,

which was crowded and distracting" (Swami 1994b: 149). So, Sai Baba kept him in solitude for nine months. Kakasaheb obeyed Sai Baba's orders strictly. He regularly read the tenth skanda of the *Bhagawat* and the eleventh skanda of *Eknath Bhagawat* which Sai Baba called *Brindavan Pothi* (Swami 1994b: 150). Kakasaheb also studied other books and discussed them with devotees in the wada.[33]

Description of many important incidents that took place in the Dixit wada can be found in *Shri Sai Satcharita* and other publications. In 1912, Krishnarao Jogeshwar Bhisma, while lying in the verandah of the wada, had the idea of celebrating Ramnavami, which became one of the biggest festivals in Shirdi.[34] Muktaram, a famous devotee of Sai Baba, died in this wada in 1919.[35] When in this wada, Bapusaheb Buti received a dream command from Sai Baba to build a wada and Shama, who was sleeping there also had a similar vision. This led to the construction of the Buti wada.[36]

Sai Baba's devotees were welcome to stay in Dixit wada. When Bade Baba, a Muslim fakir, wanted to stay in Shirdi to be near Sai Baba, no villager offered a place to him in their house. However, Dixit gladly gave a portion of his wada to Bade Baba.[37]

As a gracious host, Kakasaheb requested Upasani Maharaj to have meals in the wada and Upasani willingly became his guest. A mess was run at the wada and many people, including Upasani Maharaj, were fed free, at Kaka's expense.[38]

There is an interesting anecdote about the entry and exit of a snake in this wada.

> On another occasion, some persons were sitting in the upper floor of Kakasaheb's wada, just before nightfall, when a serpent crept through a hole in the window-frame and sat coiled up. A light was brought. Though it was first dazzled, yet it sat still and moved its head up and down. Then many

persons rushed there with sticks and cudgels, but as it sat in an awkward place, no blow could be dealt. But hearing the noises of men, the serpent went out hastily through the same hole. Then all the persons present there felt relieved.

Gunaji 2002: 119

After Sai Baba's Mahasamadhi, Shama, a close, local devotee of Sai Baba, managed the Dixit wada. He stayed in the wada and looked after the welfare of the devotees.[39]

Kakasaheb bequeathed a part of the wada to the Sansthan before his demise on 5th July 1926 and later the whole building was given to the Sansthan. In 1933, the heirs of Dixit gave part of the wada to the Sansthan[40] after which this wada was used as prasadalaya of the Shri Saibaba Sansthan, Shirdi. Because of shortage of space, a hall was built on the southern side of the wada in 1950, which was used as a prasadalaya till 1980.[41] Later the wada became a tea canteen for some years[42] (photograph 5.9a). Presently, it is being used as a museum. The rooms adjacent to this hall, which were earlier used as reading rooms, are now used as first-aid centre and blood donation centre.

An interesting incident took place in the wada. Every day in the evening, the aarti of Sai Baba's photo kept in Dixit wada was done. When Shama vacated the Dixit wada and went back to live in his own house, he took away the photo given by Sai Baba to Kakasaheb, Sai Baba's padukas and Sai Baba's idol with him. This was not acceptable to the Sansthan and the devotees. They wanted these items back and Shama agreed to return them. Therefore, on 2nd January 1940, a procession moved from Shama's house to Dixit wada carrying the items. S.B. Dhumal brought his own car for carrying the items back to Dixit wada with all the pomp and show.[43]

Photograph 5.9a: Dixit wada (tea canteen)
Source – *Shirdi Darshan*

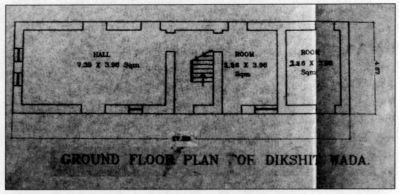

Photograph 5.9b: Old Dixit wada's layout (Ground Floor) as in 1996
Source – Shri Saibaba Sansthan Trust, Shirdi

Navalkar Wada

Navalkar wada was created within the premises of Sathe wada. Hence, in this book it is dealt as a part of the Sathe wada. On 30th September 1924, the Sathe wada was purchased by R.S. Navalkar and from that time it was known as Navalkar wada, for it was the practice to call the wadas by the names of the owner (photograph 5.10).

Photograph 5.10: Navalkar wada
Source – *Shirdi Darshan*

R.A. Tarkhad had published a report in *Shri Sai Leela* about the purchase by Navalkar after receiving information from a friend.

> Once for a Guru Purnima Utsav, Shri Ramkrishna Shrikrishna Navalkar came to Shirdi along with Shri Anandrao Shamrao Prabhakar, his friend and Baba's old devotee. They kept their luggage in the diwan-khana located on the first floor of Dixit wada and went for bath. On return, they found that their entire luggage was lying on floor in the open space

at the ground floor of the wada. Seeing this, Navalkar and Prabhakar hired another nearby room on rent, put their luggage in it and went for Baba's Darshan. Dixit Saheb was also there but he did not know about the incidence. Seeing them Sai Baba asked, "Kya Re – Could you get a place to stay?" "Yes Baba, with your blessings, we could get a place." After some time, Navalkar, with the help of Dixit, purchased the wada from Sathe. He then realized the meaning of Sai Baba's words asking him for a place of stay.

Shri Sai Leela Issue 7, 1933: 18, self-translated

Initially, the entire ground floor of the Navalkar wada was given on rent, while the first floor was kept for Navalkar himself. However, on the request of the Sansthan, a room on the first floor was allotted for the devotees to stay.[44] After the death of R.S. Navalkar, his heirs gave the wada to the Shri Saibaba Sansthan Trust, Shirdi, in 1939. Being in a bad condition, this wada was demolished completely and a new structure, consisting of four double rooms, was constructed. This new building was situated on the eastern side of the neem tree, adjacent to the Buti wada and was completed in 1941.

The Sansthan was concerned with the possession of the wada in order to preserve the Gurusthan, which was earlier inside this wada.

After the death of Shri Ramkrishna Srikrishna Navalkar, the Navalkar wada is now in a dilapidated state and is about to fall. In this wada, Samadhi of Sai Baba's beloved Guru, the neem tree under which Sai Baba used to sit when he came to Shirdi, Sai Baba's Padukas underneath the neem tree, Sai Baba's large photo opposite to Sai Baba's Paduka, Small Shiv Pindi and Nandi are present. For the purpose of their preservation, Sansthan wanted to take possession of this wada and so they were following up with the heirs of Navalkar's since two years in order to purchase the land. But nothing worked out yet. Suddenly, with Sai Baba's Grace, the heirs have, on their own, donated the entire wada to the Sansthan. wada is very fragile in a rundown & dilapidated state. Sansthan Committee has now decided to pull it down and reconstruct a wada with a double story building for pilgrims to stay. . . . Cost for the makeover is Rs. 8,000–10,000 approx., it is urged to the devotees to contribute in large amounts to this cause.

Shri Sai Leela Issue 1–3, 1939: 3, self-translated

It is also stated that Sansthan with an active effort of Nagesh Atmaram Sawant, got a building constructed with 4 double rooms between neem tree and Sathe wada with Mongolian tiles.

Aher 2017: 155, self-translated

The rooms were serial numbered 31, 32, 33 and 34.[45] Room 31 had Public Relations Officer (PRO) office and 34 was for Swami Sharnanand.[46] It is also mentioned that the marriage of Narke's son was held in Navalkar wada.[47]

The Neem Tree and the Gurusthan inside the Sathe Wada

Today, neither Sathe wada nor Navalkar wada are there. However, the neem tree, the platform surrounding it and the hidden cave of Sai Baba's guru exist.

Initially, during Sai Baba's stay in Shirdi, Sai Baba's photograph was placed in the Gurusthan in a small built-up area inside the Sathe wada, where aarti used to be performed by Bapusaheb Jog twice a day.

In the year 1941, as the Navalkar wada came under the possession of the Sansthan, a chatri was built on the platform of the neem tree and a marble slab was placed on Sai Baba's guru's hidden cave. Megha's Shivling, Nandi and Sai Baba's photo were moved adjacent to this marble slab.[48]

Later, on the Guru Purnima of 1974, an idol of Sai Baba in the posture of sitting on the stone, which was about three feet in height, was kept on the marble platform. It was donated by Yashwantrao D. Dave and sculpted by Harish Balaji Talim, the son of Balaji Vasant Talim.[49]

As the original photo placed near padukas was getting old, a new photo by Narayanrao Devhare was placed by the Sansthan trustee Vasantrao Narayan Gorakshkar on the third day of Shri Sai Baba's punyatithi, that is, 30th September 1952.[50]

Photograph 5.11: Old Gurusthan and neem tree

According to another version, earlier there was Sai Baba's statue inside the old Gurusthan. Below this statue was an opening to the cave. Sai Baba wanted to close this place and therefore it was closed by placing Sai Baba's statue over it. (photograph 5.11 and 5.12) Before Sai Baba's statue, Akkalkot Maharaj's marble padukas[51] were kept to cover the place. Now the whereabouts of these padukas are not known.

Photograph 5.12: Inside old Gurusthan

Presently, the neem tree and the items on the platform have become a covered area. This place is worshipped by the temple priests on a daily basis in a routine manner.

This place is a major attraction and is visited by almost all the visitors.

According to another version, renovation of Gurusthan was done on 11th July 2007, and the platform on which Sai Baba's padukas were installed and Sanskrit shloka written by Shri Upasani Maharaj, has been removed.[52] We can see that Sai Baba's idol which was earlier placed in Gurusthan is not there now.[53]

Renovation of the Wadas by the Shri Saibaba Sansthan

As the condition of the wadas, in particular the Navalkar wada, deteriorated, the Sansthan took the initiative of renovating them. The work of renovation started in Shirdi on 25th June 1941, which was the auspicious day of Akshay Tritiya.

Work went on simultaneously in the Dixit wada, Buti wada and the Samadhi Mandir. The floor, the plaster of the walls and the bathroom of the three rooms in the Dixit wada were constructed. After this work ended, the Navalkar wada's construction resumed again in the Bhadrapad month. The work of making a canopy under the neem tree, the construction of four adjacent rooms on the eastern side and frames of the windows of the Sathe wada had also started. People who attended the festivals of Guru Purnima and Shri Sai Punyatithi (Vijayadashami) saw this work of renovation. By the end of the month of Kartik, the work of the rooms had finished.[54]

Contributions for the renovation of the Navalkar wada were made by Dr. G.P. Desai, Dr. Rajgopal Chari, Nagesh Atmaram Sawant and Bhaskar Sadashiv Satam.

He estimated Rs. 10-12 thousand expense, but they could collect only Rs. 500 till now. Out of this Rs. 500, Rs. 100 came from Dr. G.P. Desai from Rangoon and some contribution from the devotees of Madras. Dr. Rajgopal Chari from Nellore collected Rs. 102. . . . An old devotee from Mumbai, sub-inspector Nagesh Atmaram Sawant and his colleague Bhaskar Sadashiv Satam wished to give Rs. 101 and Rs. 501 on the occasion of Baba's Punnay Tithi.

Shri Sai Leela Issue 8, 1940: 312, self-translated

Adjacent to the Navalkar wada, on 6th October 1941 (Aher 2017), during the period of renovation, the Sansthan purchased a piece of land from Shri Ramchandra Dada Patil. After the clearance of debris, this land became a part of the wada area. With the permission of Buti, a second door for the entry and exit of devotees to Sai Baba's Samadhi was created. A drain was built on both sides of Dixit wada in order to maintain hygiene. A window was constructed in room number 3 for extra sunlight. The floors were plastered and a bathroom was constructed in room number 2. Nearing the festival of Datta jayanti, the work of painting of eight rooms of Navalkar wada was completed.[55]

These wadas were closely linked with the growth of the Sai movement for about a decade prior to the Mahasamadhi of Sai Baba as well as for many years thereafter. Of all the wadas, only Dixit wada is of symbolic use as a part of it has been converted into a museum which contains some of the items that belonged to Sai Baba. However, not many people visit it. Hence, it is desirable that the museum is upgraded. In view of the sanctity of Dixit wada due to its existence before Sai Baba's Mahasamadhi, it is desirable that it is fully restored and developed as a heritage structure.

*****

Notes

1. *Sainath Prabha* (Kiran 1, 1916: 2(i)).
2. Swami (2006: 120).
3. Gunaji (2002: 21, 22).
4. Swami (2006: 112).
5. Swami (1994c: 551).
6. *Sainath Prabha* (Kiran 2, 1916: 33).

7. Swami (1994c: 106).
8. Ambekar (1997: 131).
9. *Shri Sai Leela* (Issue 1, 2, 1930: 1).
10. When Upasani Maharaj first came to Shirdi, He stayed in Dixit wada. That day, some of the devotees were going to Dwarkamayi for Sai Baba's darshan and requested Upasani Maharaj to come with them. They came out of Dixit wada and entered the Sathe wada through its front gate and came out from the 2nd gate which is a back gate on Dwarkamayi Road. This indicates that there were two gates in the Sathe wada (Dikshit undated: 5).
11. Shri Sai Baba's flower garden encompassed the area covered by Sathe wada plus Buti wada and a small portion of Dixit wada and extended up to Dwarkamayi (Gunaji 2002: 22).
12. It is mentioned in *Shri Sai Leela* that Sai Baba told Kakasaheb Dixit that in this place there is a turbat of a peer. When it was excavated they found a turbat there. Sai Baba told Kakasaheb that "'this is my father's place' and asked him to light perfumed sticks on every Thursday and Friday and you will be benefitted" (*Shri Sai Leela* Issue 1, 1923: 11–12).
13. *Shri Sai Leela* (Issue 6, 7, 8, 1927: 729).
14. Khaparde (undated: 14).
15. Swami (2006: 116); Swami (2004: 554–555).
16. *Sainathne Sharne* (Gujarati): 375.
17. *Shri Sai Leela* (Issue 1, 1923: 17).
18. Kher (2013: 35, 146).
19. *Shri Sai Leela* (Issue 6–9, 1935: 22).
20. Swami (1994b: 144).
21. *Shri Sai Leela* (Issue 6–9, 1935: 33).
22. Dabholkar (1930: 859).
23. Dabholkar (1930: 90).
24. *Shri Sai Leela* (Issue 6–9, 1935: 38).
25. Gokhale (2004: 51).
26. Kher (2013: 69).
27. "In the Dixit wada, the first floor was spacious with Sai Baba's photo and it was this place where daily Puja and Aarti were conducted. In the ground floor, there was a general hall for the

devotees. There were rooms on the ground floor for devotees with family. At the backside of the ground floor, rooms were given to those who would cook for themselves, which helped many. Ever since this wada came up, most of the pilgrims preferred to stay here, hence the ground floor general hall and the family rooms were found occupied always. Kakasaheb would stay on the first floor and his close associates taking the rooms on the first floor. Rest all, would come on the first floor only when Kaka used to recite Pothi or during the Aarti. There was a rule that no ladies would be allowed on the first floor. Kaka used to sit on the right-hand side of Sai Baba's photo and would sleep there only" (*Shri Sai Leela* Issue 6–9, 1935: 44).

28. *Shri Sai Leela* (Issue 8 1932, Year 9: 13). Anubhav mentions: Shri Shamrao Ramchandra Jaykar in his experience has stated that, in the year 1916, M.W. Pradhan had sent him to Shirdi to get Portrait of Baba. Though the contract was for one portrait, he prepared three portraits of Baba in three different poses. He took them to M.W. Pradhan and gave him all the three. But Pradhan accepted two and accordingly paid for two but returned the third to Shamrao, who then took it to Baba. Baba laughed and then asked Shama to give this Photo to Kaka for keeping in his bungalow in the living area.

29. *Shri Sai Leela* (Issue 1, 1924: 126).

30. *Shri Sai Leela* (Issue 11–12, 1931: 25–26).

31. *Shri Sai Leela* (Issue 1, 1933: 4).

32. *Shri Sai Leela* (Issue 8, 1940: 307).

33. Gunaji (1944: 34).

34. Swami (1994: 103); Gunaji (2002: 34–35).

35. *Sainath Prabha* (1919: 25).

36. Gunaji (2002: 210–211).

37. *Shri Sai Leela* (2008: 32).

38. Swami (2002: 360).

39. *Shri Sai Leela* (1939: 113–114).

40. Aher (2017: 144–145).

41. Chitluri (2000: 53).

42. *Shri Sai Leela* (Issue 10–12, 1939: 113).

43. *Shri Sai Leela* (Issue 1, 1933: 4).

44. Interview of Baba Jagtap – born in Shirdi in 1947, his father was immediately transferred after his birth but the family again came back to Shirdi after 5-6 years and since then is associated with the Sansthan.

45. *Shri Sai Leela* (1941: 407).

46. *Shri Sai Leela* (Issue 7–10, 1941: 400).

47. *Shri Sai Leela* (Issue 7–10, 1941: 407).

48. Chitluri (2012: 20).

49. *Shri Sai Leela* (Issue 4, 1952: 56).

50. Gunaji (2002: 26–27).

51. Aher (2017: 46).

52. *Shri Sai Leela* (Issue 7–10 1941: 406).

53. *Shri Sai Leela* (Issue 7–10 1941: 405, self-translated).

54. *Shri Sai Leela* (Issue 7–10, 1941: 406).

6

Buti Wada, Now the Samadhi Mandir of Shri Sai Baba

This chapter illustrates the process through which Shrimant Gopalrao Mukund Buti constructed Buti wada, now the Samadhi Mandir, and the years of care that Shri Sai Baba took in developing the land on which it was built. It also touches on the formation of the Shri Saibaba Sansthan Trust, Shirdi.

> Baba [n]ever made any fuss about the things, which He wanted to accomplish, but He so skilfully arranged the circumstances that the people were surprised at the slow but sure results attained. The construction of the Samadhi Mandir is an instance.
>
> Gunaji 2002: 210

Sai Baba's Command to Shrimant Gopalrao Mukund Buti: Build a Wada to Fulfil the Desire of Everyone

Gopalrao Mukund Buti, also known as Shrimant Bapusaheb Buti, was a multi-millionaire from Nagpur and a devotee of Shri Gajanan Maharaj of Shegaon. He was brought to Shirdi by S.B. Dhumal, an advocate from Nasik, in 1910 (*Shri Sai Leela* Issue 5, 1940: 212). Buti often visited Sai Baba at Shirdi with his family. One day, it occurred to him to construct a house in Shirdi for himself (Gunaji 2002: 210). Sometime later, when he was sleeping at Dixit wada in Shirdi, Sai Baba appeared in his dream and commanded him to build a wada, with an attached temple, for his own use. Sleeping near him was Shama who also had a similar vision. On waking up, both exchanged notes and became emotional and motivated. Shama narrated the dream vision in which Shri Sai Baba asked him to build a wada in order to fulfil the desire of everyone. Since he was a multi-millionaire and money was not a problem, Buti immediately decided to build the wada. He and Shama prepared a plan and got it approved from Kakasaheb Dixit, who was also present there. When the proposal was submitted to Sai Baba, he approved it then and there.

> Baba came to him and ordered distinctly: Build the wada with the temple! I shall fulfil the desires of all.
>
> Gunaji 2002: 210

Photograph 6.1 Old Buti wada

The Strong Foundation of Buti Wada: Constructed on Land Ploughed and Nurtured by Shri Sai Baba for Several Years

When asked about the auspicious time to begin laying the foundation of the wada, Sai Baba confirmed that the moment itself was suitable. Shama immediately broke a coconut to mark the auspicious moment and the construction work began (Kher 2014: 657).

Sai Baba had ploughed the land and planted a flower garden where the present Samadhi mandir stands. He would carry pots full of water on his shoulders and water the plants regularly. The flowers like marigold and jasmine that he sowed and their leaves were freely distributed to the various Hindu temples and the holy places of the Muslims without distinction (Swami 1994a: 19). The land, bordering the village boundary including the one on which Buti had his building was owned by Hari Sitaram Dixit. Later, the required land was donated to the Shri Saibaba Sansthan Trust by the sons of Dixit and Buti (*Shri Sai Leela* Issue 8, 1923: 52).

> I own a piece of land at Shirdi on a portion of which my friend the late Gopal Mukund alias Bapusaheb Buti has put up a structure with my content. I intend to transfer that land to the trustees of the Shirdi Sansthan for the use and benefit of that Sansthan. If I happen to die without transferring the said the land to the said trustees, my executors should transfer the same to them.
>
> *Shri Sai Leela,* Issue 11–12, 1931: 25

> The land on the village boundary owned by Hari Sitaram Dixit, on which Shree Gopal Mukund Buti constructed his Wada was donated to the Sansthan by Shree Dixit and Shree Buti's sons.
>
> *Shri Sai Leela* Issue 8, Shirdi Sansthan
> 1st Annual Report, 1923: 52, self-translated

The construction of the ground floor, the basement and a well behind the wada were all completed under Shama's supervision. Sai Baba also suggested a few changes on his way to Lendi from Dwarkamayi and back (Kher 2014: 655).

Buti also thought that in the ground floor there should be an open room (platform), at the centre of which the idol of Lord Krishna, holding a flute, should be installed. When asked, Sai Baba permitted it. Hence, it was decided that the middle portion of the building will be a temple and, around it, a residential area would be constructed.

What his devotees did not know then, was that Sai Baba himself would become Murlidhar as his shrine would be located in this place.

> Samadhi shrine is in the centre of that house, and all outlying parts are used as accession thereto. This building must have cost a lakh of rupees.
>
> Swami 1994c: 89

Workers called from Nagpur had to leave the temple's construction midway due to certain reasons and therefore the construction had to be suspended. However, the construction of the residential area was continued (*Shri Sai Leela* Issue 7, 1923: 60).

Formation of Shri Saibaba Sansthan Trust for Development of the Samadhi Mandir

After Sai Baba's Mahasamadhi, between the years 1918 to 1922, Shirdi became a comparatively quiet place. The number of visitors declined. However, ritualistic worship of Sai Baba continued (Gokhale 2004: 73; Aher 2017: 101–104). The sadhus, bairagis and fakirs started leaving Shirdi. Wherever free food and water is available, crowds will gather. This is how the society functions. Before Sai Baba took Samadhi, many people used to get monthly salary from him but after his Mahasamadhi, this distribution of money stopped. Hence, many of them left Shirdi (Gokhale 2004: 68).

During the four years from 1918 to 1922, Sai Baba's Samadhi could not be well looked after. For example, Sai Baba's Samadhi was given a bath only once in eight days. In 1922 Kakasaheb Dixit came to Shirdi. After seeing his Guru's Samadhi in such a bad state, he felt unhappy and came up with the idea of creation of Shri Saibaba Sansthan Trust.

After due deliberation, Shri Saibaba Sansthan Trust, Shirdi was formed in 1922. "Permission for the management of the Shirdi Sansthan was approved by Ahmednagar District Court on 13th February 1922" (*Shri Sai Leela* Issue 8, 1923: 50). The first meeting of the Sansthan Committee was held on 6th April 1922 which was Ramnavami day (*Shri Sai Leela* Issue 8, 1923: 50). In the meeting many vital decisions were taken. After Sai Baba's Samadhi, his clothes, watch, chillum and padukas were to be kept in the Masjid. His mattress, copper, silver and brass utensils and his expensive clothes were to be placed in the Samadhi Mandir. The remaining small items were to be stored in the Chawadi (*Shri Sai Leela* Issue 8, 1923: 52). The suggestions of the sons of Gopalrao Buti to cover Sai Baba's Samadhi with marble and to pave the floor of sabha mandap were accepted (*Shri Sai Leela* Issue 5, 1924: 123).

The Samadhi was given the form of turbat and there was enough space around the turbat to do pradakshina (Gokhale 2004: 67). After a few years, this pit was filled, levelled and marble was overlaid on the platform. A marble slab of the same size as Sai Baba's Samadhi was placed over the marble floor and today this is the Samadhi we see.

Structurally speaking, the Samadhi and Sai Baba's idol are on a square platform with a grill around. The Samadhi is 6 feet long and 2 feet wide. Surrounding it is an altar 9 feet by 9 feet, with a height of 3 feet. Three steps lead to this altar (*Shri Sai Leela* 1981: 27).

According to Pramod Aher, "Samadhi's length is 6 ft 8 inches and breadth is 2 ft 10 inches. It is placed in the middle of the platform lying North and South. The dimensions of the marble platform are 11 ft 10 inches by 11 ft 9 inches in length and breadth and 2 ft 4 inches in height" (Aher 2017: 103).

In 1996, the dimensions of the platform around the marble Samadhi were 12 ft 2 inches by 10 ft 1 inch, the height being 33 inches approximately (photograph 6.2).

Thus, there is a variation between the dimensions mentioned in *Shri Sai Leela*, those given by Aher and the measurements in 1996. It is possible that over a period of time the dimensions changed due to repairs and extensions.

Photograph 6.2: Old Samadhi Mandir (inside Buti Wada) with
inscription written on the steps
Source – *Shirdi Darshan*

On the third step these words are inscribed:
"Shri Sai Baba hay miti Ashwin Shudh 10 roj mangalwar tarikh 15 October, 1918 roji samadhist jhale."
[Shri Sai Baba took Samadhi on tenth day in Shukl Paksh of Ashwin, Tuesday, 15th Oct 1918.]

This is inscribed in Marathi on the central portion of the step. On either side there are Urdu inscriptions also.

The sanctum sanctorum of the Samadhi Mandir on the ground floor is 45 ft by 21 ft and extends from the door behind the Samadhi to the grill arch. The area from the Sabha Mandap grill to the old Nandi entrance gate is called the Madhya Mandap (38 ft by 36 ft). An oblique area of 69,492 sq. ft lies behind this up to Vyas Peeth. There are five rooms on each side of the Samadhi on the ground floor. The first floor has six rooms on the north and four on the south side (Aher 2017: 101–104).

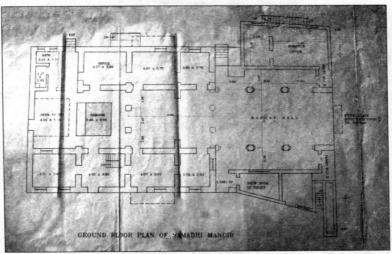

Photograph 6.3: Samadhi Mandir layout (Ground Floor) as in 1996
Source – Shri Saibaba Sansthan Trust, Shirdi

Development of the Samadhi Mandir Complex

The land of Buti wada was within the village boundary. Part of this land was owned by Buti and part by Dixit. Initially, the building was constructed on this land. Later, from 19th September 1919, this place was rented at ₹11 per year for 50 years. This is recorded in Office of Land records (Aher 2017: 101–104).

After spending a large amount of money to build the wada in the year 1917, Buti finally handed it over to Shri Saibaba Sansthan Trust, Shirdi. If it was an expenditure of one lakh rupees in 1917, one can imagine the value of it today. Buti wada in Shirdi was almost identical to Buti's own wada at Nagpur. There was no plaque, signboard or nameplate proclaiming the name of Buti in the temple. However, some time ago, the Sansthan put up a plaque in his name at the entrance of the Samadhi Mandir.

Photograph 6.4 depicts an inscription behind the entry door.

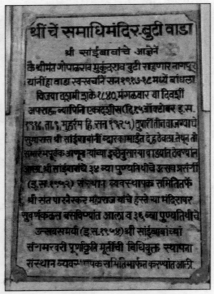

Photograph 6.4: Inscription written behind the door of the Samadhi Mandir – Buti wada

[According to the command of Shri Sai Baba, late Shrimant Gopalrao Mukundrao Buti, resident of Nagpur, constructed this wada between the years 1917–1918 at his own expense. On the day of Vijayadashami Shaka 1840, Tuesday afternoon, Vyapini Ekadasi day (15th October 1918, 9 day Moharram Hijri year 1925) afternoon at approximately 3 p.m., Shri Sai Baba left his body in Dwarkamayi. From there, with his wish, his body was brought to this wada ceremoniously. On the 34 Punyatithi of Shri Sai Baba (year 1952) the Sansthan Management Committee, by the hand of Saint Shri Parnerkar Maharaj, installed the Golden Kalash atop this temple, and on the 36 Punyatithi (year 1954) the life-size marble statue of Shri Sai Baba was installed with all rites and rituals by the Sansthan Management Committee. Self-translated]

Inside the Samadhi Mandir, photographs of the most dedicated and staunch devotees during Sai Baba's time, such as Nanasaheb Chandorkar, Annasaheb Dabholkar, Balasaheb Bhate, Nanasaheb Nimonkar, Bapusaheb Buti, Mahalsapati Bhagat, Bayjabai Kote Patil, Kakasaheb Dixit, Tatya Ganpati Kote Patil, Dasganu, Annasaheb Dabholkar, Bhagoji Shinde, Kashiram Bala Shimpi, Laxman Ganesh Noolkar, Laxmibai Shinde, Madhavrao Deshpande and Moreshwar Pradhan (photograph 6.5), are put up for the future generations to remember (*Shri Sai Leela* Issue 1–2, 1930: 2). It appears that more photographs were added later. Any visitor in the queue for Sai Baba's darshan can see the photographs.

Photograph 6.5: Photographs of devotees inside the Samadhi Mandir

Devotees and visitors are permitted to enter the Buti wada during scheduled hours to pay homage to Sai Baba in his tomb and attend his aartis. The Samadhi and the statue of Sai Baba are worshipped by the devotees in the traditional Hindu method of worship. Every day, four major aartis are performed in the temple. Other ritualistic practices are also carried on as scheduled. Besides, many festivals and religious activities are performed throughout the year as per the well-established puja calendar of the temple.

*****

7

Dakshina Bhiksha Sanstha (1915–1921)
(The First Sanstha of Shirdi)

This chapter narrates the origin, functions and contributions of Dakshina Bhiksha Sanstha created by Rao Bahadur Hari Vinayak Sathe in pursuance of the wishes of Shri Sai Baba of Shirdi to create a proper management system in Shirdi.

Starting from a humble beginning as an unknown fakir and at times disrespected by the urchins and some villagers as a person with eccentric traits, the real spiritual personality of Sai Baba slowly unfolded over the decades during his stay in the remote village of Shirdi.

At the initial stage, during the second half of the nineteenth century, the young Sai Baba was looked-after by Ganapati Kote Patil and his wife Bayjabai Kote Patil. Other devotees like Kashiram Bala Shimpi, Mhalsapati Chimnaji Nagare, Nanasaheb Chandorkar, Shama, Sagunameru Naik and a few others who either belonged to Shirdi or visited him from the neighbouring villages like Nimgaon and Rahata, served him in numerous ways. Sai Baba's needs were minimal and he lived a frugal life. He begged food from five houses[1] on a daily basis, collected oil from the shops to light lamps and stayed in a dilapidated mosque called Dwarkamayi. His other needs were a few pieces of kafni, patka, chillums and tobacco, a satka, a few cooking utensils and some rags used as his bed. These were all that he possessed.[2]

At the initial stage, the lodging and other requirements of the devotees who visited Sai Baba were also taken care by some local devotees like Bayaji Appa Kote Patil, Shama, Mhalsapati, Appa Jagale and Kashiram Shimpi. True to their Indian culture, they delighted in taking care of the fakirs, sadhus and mendicants visiting their village. However, during the first decade of the twentieth century, particularly from the year 1908 onwards, Sai Baba's influence, particularly over the people of Maharashtra, both urban and rural, increased exponentially (Swami 1994b: 13). His devotees believed him to be a true fakir who possessed miraculous powers and his fame spread through word-of-mouth. Kirtankars also spread Sai Baba's glory in the religious congregations and festivals that they attended. Ganpatrao Dattatreya Sahasrabuddhe, popularly called Dasganu, was one such famous kirtankar of Maharashtra, who was in the police department as a Constable for some time.[3] This drew many rich, powerful and influential people, including government officials, lawyers, businessmen and educated persons from Mumbai and other urban areas of Maharashtra, besides the rural folk, to Shirdi.[4] As a consequence, the number and the quality of activities pertaining to Sai Baba also multiplied rapidly. During this time, at the behest of the earnest devotees, Sai Baba started spending alternate nights in Chawadi and Dwarkamayi. This obviously worked as a good arrangement as devotees who wished to maintain Dwarkamayi in a clean and sanitized manner could do so. Also some constructions that were needed could be undertaken.

> In addition to this daily pooja and aarti of the day, while Shree Baba retires, every alternate night, to an adjoining Chavady, for his nights' stay, as has been usual with Him for many years.
>
> *Sainath Prabha* Kiran 1, 1916: 11

Devotees worshipped him at the Chawadi from 10th December 1909. His movement to and from these two places took the shape of a mirthful procession, full of fanfare, drum beats and accompanied by hundreds of devotees.[5] Thus, regular and congregational worship of Sai Baba began from the year 1910,[6] following the prescribed Hindu rites and rituals. According to one commentator, the change in form of worship had started from 1908.[7] Henceforth, each and every action of Sai Baba at Shirdi turned into an event that created a festive and vibrant atmosphere. Devotees tried to create an aura of royalty and opulence around him as is done in the case of Hindu deities and Hindu royalty. One ardent and widowed devotee, by the name of Sunderabai Ksheersagar popularly called Radhakrishna Ayi, collected articles of worship and paraphernalia for the Chawadi procession[8] like palki (palanquin), simhasana (throne), chhata (umbrella), chamara (hand-fan) and morchal (hand fan made of peacock feathers), gold and silver necklaces and other costly decorative items. These were procured by some of the affluent devotees of Sai Baba at her behest.[9] Sai Baba was most dissatisfied with such paraphernalia. He never used the throne or the palanquin, shunning the numerous pleadings of the devotees.

When Sai Baba arrived in Shirdi, the population was around 1,000.[10] As mentioned in chapter 5, by April 1916, the population of Shirdi was about 1,500.[11] Sai Baba was like a one-man institution, but even an institution needs a proper system of management to run it smoothly. By the beginning of the second decade of the last century, the team of devotees (both resident and visiting), like Tatya, Nanasaheb Chandorkar, Kakasaheb Dixit, Balasaheb Bhate, Shama, Anna Chinchinkar, Bapusaheb Jog, Gopalrao Mukund Buti, Mhalsapati and others had engaged themselves fully in the management of the affairs of Sai Baba in an informal manner.

Shri Sai Baba's Glory and Influx of Visitors: Need for a Management System

Given the heavy influx of visitors, the need for a better organized and systematic instrument to handle the crowd became essential. The situation needed more persons, a better skill-set and better attitudes from the sevakari and other devotees who ran the show. By 1910, the numbers of people, demands and problems had increased.[12] Unfortunately, the much-needed upgradation of the system to contain the problems and manage the complex situation had not been conceived even though many devotees were government officers and lawyers of the High Court of Bombay. No one dared to interfere in the prevailing situation controlled by Sai Baba. They were individually serving Shri Sai Baba according to their wishes. Sai Baba allowed each devotee to serve him in his own way and did not tolerate interference by any devotee with the ways of any other devotee. Most of the visiting or resident devotees were dedicated to serve the Guru according to his desire. For them, Sai Baba's sayings were the words of judgement on each and every issue.

Nevertheless, some sort of a crisis slowly started building up given the lack of a proper system to take care of the material aspects of a spiritual colossus like Sai Baba. He believed in the concept of rinanubandha as expounded in many Hindu scriptures, including Shri Geeta.

Rinanubandha is the prenatal ties and obligations or the ties of kinship and the irresistible pull of destiny or connections with innumerable people of former lives after one enters a new birth.[13] An anecdote in *Shri Sai Satcharita* explains the concept in a proper perspective. Once, Sai Baba purchased two goats at an exorbitant cost of ₹16 each, whereas the actual price of each goat was ₹2 to ₹4. When asked about this unreasonably high payment, Sai Baba directed the curious devotees to feed the goats with a seer of pulses each and return them to the owner. This was in addition to the money already paid to the owner. According to the market principle of sale and purchase, the amount was ridiculously high. However, as per Sai Baba, he did so because of obligations to the goats carried forward from a past life and also the past obligation among the two goats.[14] This is a concept that the western world would find difficult to accept. Perhaps, there is more to faith than reason can tell.

Such mystical explanation could not be understood in its correct perspective by people with mundane attitude. Some staunch devotees followed the concept of rinanubandha in letter and spirit. On the other hand, some dishonest and manipulative persons took advantage of Sai Baba's kindness. They held that as disciples they had the prerogative to give and take such dakshina in relation to the Guru. They would not tolerate any interference in this matter. A few of them even played various tricks, including sentimentalizing trivial issues to extract money from Sai Baba on some pretext or the other. Some became boisterous in their demands and quarrelled in front of Sai Baba.

The compassionate Sai Baba tolerated this nuisance for long but, at times, reproved them for not being ethical in their conduct. In spite of many admonitions, there was no qualitative improvement in the situation. Sai Baba expressed his exasperation in Marathi language to some of his close devotees:

Shreemant aani laakhpati asel tar tyala yethen yeun basun vyavastha karu de. Hya lokana paisa vaatun laagale mhanaje samjel! Mi ithoon uthoon baaher jaaun basato! Paisa kuthun aanu aani kuthparyantdeun? Paise det naahin mahanun bhatashi kaay maramari karaaychi kin kaay?

Sainath Prabha Kiran 1, 1916: 28

[Whether they are rich and millionaires, then also they will come and make arrangements at this place. They will understand (appreciate) only when they will distribute money to these people. Let me get up from here and sit outside. Where from do I get the money and how far can I distribute! If I can't give money, will you keep flocking the Bhatts in front of me?]

The Problem: Rising Donations and Greedy Beneficiaries

Collections from donations increased and also the greed of the beneficiaries. Mundane considerations overtook their ethical conduct.

Sai Baba reared and protected his devotees with love and kindness. Even when admonishing them, he would not shun them or stop giving them benefits like money, food, shelter and other items.

An article captioned "How unpleasant societies and their troubles developed" published in *Sainath Prabha* (*Sainath Prabha* Kiran 1, 1916: 14), a magazine brought out by the Dakshina Bhiksha Sanstha (D.B.S.) from Shirdi, brings to the fore the problems escalating around Sai Baba during those days. This article written by Sundarrao Narayan is summarized here:

A group of motivated individuals indulged in frequent quarrels, manipulated naivedya items from Shri Sai Baba by pushing the children to the front, extorted money on various pretexts and displayed impertinent behaviour that disturbed the peace around Shri Sai Baba.

Such unbearable annoyances and unutterable disturbances were hourly committed by such constituents of the vicious characters that even Shree Sai Daya-Moorty's frequent reprimands now and then seemed to be powerless to mend matters. The poor bhaktas, found perhaps in their helpless condition, no effective salvation; much less the confused villagers, who but gaped wildly with wondering eyes!

Sainath Prabha Kiran 1, 1916: 15

Sundarrao Narayan further states that:

> As bhavic people from the surroundings approached Him,
> for relief of their ailments, in course of time, and offered
> copper coins and silver bits, as Dakshinas, He often refused
> to accept them, allowing them to lie before Him, until
> they were collected by evenings and utilised by His few
> devotees for sundry charity, or, for the purchase of His
> sundry requirements, like tobacco, oil, fuel, & c. He is also
> said to have insisted, occasionally, on the visitors, offering
> their dakshinas, in copper alone, and He would not accept
> silver bits, much less full rupees. Subsequently, it is said,
> Shree Baba, while he was often alone, without His trusted
> associates began accumulating Dakshina coppers Himself,
> till their disposal as aforesaid. Thus, from copper to silver
> bits and rupees in succession, developed the system of His
> accepting Dakshinas, or arpans, from His increased devotees.
> It needs mention here, that these were purely voluntary
> arpans from His devotees. It was from a very recent date,
> probably, since about fifteen years ago, and, as the bulk of
> His admirers began pouring in, with a remarkably rapid
> succession, that Shree Sai Nath is said to have started asking
> dakshinas of the visitors, on the undoubted justification
> of *"jyaanchekadun paise ghetto tyaanchyaach kaamaala te paise
> laavaton, te malaakaay karaayache?"*

Sainath Prabha Kiran 1, 1916: 18–19

[Whosoever I take money from, I utilize the money in his
cause. What have I got to do with such money? This also
means that the money he took was given away in charity
and the donor reaped benefits.]

> Such dakshina receipts range from single copper, equivalent
> to three pies, to chaulis, pauvlis, adhelis, rupees and even
> sovereigns, from each individual, often in smaller or larger
> multiples. Since about seven or eight years, perhaps, Shree
> Sai Baba asks for dakshinas in tens and hundreds, and He,
> evidently, has His reasons for so doing.

Sainath Prabha Kiran 1, 1916: 19

Even when demanding bhiksha and dakshina from some devotees, Sai Baba displayed a total sense of worldly detachment. Questioned on this, his replies were mystical and pithy.

> Such receipts, in recent years, amount to an average of one to two hundred rupees daily, and every bit of it is distributed by Shree Sai Baba Himself to various persons, for various reasons, best known to Himself.

> *Sainath Prabha* Kiran 1, 1916: 20[15]

Sai Baba was also a protector of the cows.

> *Gaay garibaachi gokhni (sanrakshan) meech karito; Chaar prahar din (diwas) va chaar prahar raatra meech sambhalaton; dusra kaun karanaar aahe.*

> *Sainath Prabha* Kiran 1, 1916: 21

[I preserve and protect the cows and the poor. I take care of them day in and day out; who else can do this?]

Some greedy and unscrupulous persons encouraged a number of petty jugglers, wrestlers, dancers and thirty-two tamashawalla[16] groups, who came from outside to perform before Shri Sai and receive lot of money. This disturbed the good and ordinary devotees.

> When ineffective suggestions from bhaktas to discontinue such scenes failed, strong remonstrations from even Shree Sai Baba seemed equally fruitless.

> *Sainath Prabha* Kiran 1, 1916: 24

An Attempt to Establish Order: The Dakshina Bhiksha Sanstha

The Dakshina Bhiksha Sanstha was conceptualized when Sai Baba, being vexed with the prevailing disturbed condition in Shirdi, called Sathe to streamline and control the situation. One day, in mid-November 1915, he let out his feelings in Marathi during the public audience:

Majhe Nana aale tar gaay garibana changale hoil aani khavyala milel, aani majhe saheb aale mhanaje sarv vyavastha neet hoil.

Sainath Prabha Kiran 1, 1916: 27

[Once my Nana (Nanasaheb Chandorkar) comes, it will be beneficial for both the poor people and the cows and they will get food, and when my Saheb (Rao Bahadur H.V. Sathe) comes, all the arrangements will be proper.]

On 1st December 1915, in his early morning durbar after meals, Sai Baba suddenly directed Anna Chinchnikar, a resident devotee of Shirdi, to write to Rao Bahadur Hari Vinayak Sathe, a retired Deputy Collector residing at Poona and one of the senior bhaktas, to come at once to Shirdi to meet him. Later at Chinchnikar's behest, Bapusaheb Jog wrote a letter to Sathe and dispatched it on the same day. On receipt of the letter on Friday, 3rd December, Sathe decided to visit Shirdi at an early date. Later, on the same day, Sathe received another letter from his father-in-law, Dada Kelkar, confirming the message of Sai Baba. Hence, Sathe rushed to Shirdi by the next available train. He reached Shirdi on 4th December 1915 (Saturday) and promptly presented himself before Sai Baba in Dwarkamayi. However, no interview took place with Sai Baba on that day. On the next day, that is, on 5th December 1915 (Sunday), at 9.30 a.m., Sathe prostrated before Sai Baba, when he was on his way from Dwarkamayi to Lendibagh[17] but no discussions took place at that time either. Later in the day, before the noon arati, when Sathe sat near Sai Baba along with some other devotees, Sai Baba told him in Marathi:

Arey saheb, tu pahatosnaa hey lok malaa traas detaat, hyanche badal tu kaahintari bandobast kara.

Sainath Prabha Kiran 2, 1916: 32–34

[Oh Saheb, you can see that these people are troubling me. Now you make some arrangements about this.]

Sathe could not immediately comprehend the purport of these words from Sai Baba as they came suddenly. Dr. Chidambaram Pillay, who was also present there, promised Sathe that he would narrate the problems to which Sai Baba referred in the afternoon. In the afternoon Dr. C. Pillay explained to Sathe that Sai Baba was referring to the deteriorating conditions at Shirdi. The problems were the manipulation and extraction of money and food items from Sai Baba on various pretexts, the mischievous role of the thirty-two tamashawalla groups and their local dalals, inconvenience caused to Sai Baba and devotees due to bickerings of these people and their impertinent behaviour, even before Sai Baba (*Sainath Prabha* Kiran 2, 1916: 34–35).

Having described the problems, Dr. C. Pillay exhorted H.V. Sathe to resolve them by saying that he had been called by Sai Baba "to arrange and establish order here for ever" (*Sainath Prabha* Kiran 2, 1916: 36).

Dr. Pillay's views were subsequently confirmed to Sathe by some devotees like Anna Chinchnikar, Raghuji Ganpat Scindia Patel, Tatya Ganpati Kote Patil, Sundarrao Narayan and so on as well. Hence Sathe immediately moved to action, in compliance with the wishes of Sai Baba.[18]

During 4th and 5th December, in order to receive the opinion and cooperation of prominent and affluent bhaktas and the common villagers of Shirdi, a letter was circulated:

> The existing unsatisfactory state of affairs in connection with Shree Sai Nath's Masjid and Chavady & c., and requesting the formation of a duly-constituted Karya Kari Mandaly.

> *Sainath Prabha* Kiran 2, 1916: 37

The circular generated response from different segments of the society. The unsympathetic responses termed the circular as "uncalled for", "impracticable" and "imposing dictatorship on the affairs of Sai Baba when he manages his own affairs".

Sympathetic replies came from a few devotees of Sai Baba who appreciated the proposal and volunteered to cooperate with Sathe to establish an order as against the prevailing state of disorder (*Sainath Prabha* Kiran 2, 1916: 37–38).

> A meeting was actually held in the evening of Wednesday, the 8th December 1915 in Mr. Dikshit's wada, sanctioned, of course, by Shree Sai Sadguru. Over two hundred people gathered on the occasion, composed of all outside bhaktas, then in Shirdi, and many of the village gentlemen, old and young.
>
> *Sainath Prabha* Kiran 2, 1916: 41

Sathe was elected the Chairman of the meeting. He proposed and constituted a council of forty-four members from among the attendees, who volunteered to perform the assigned duties. Thus, the foundation of the Dakshina Bhiksha Sanstha (D.B.S.) was laid on 8th December 1915.[19] In the meeting, the various duties needed in Sai Nath's Masjid, Chawadi and his nitya niyamas were apportioned among the attendees. From the morning of Thursday, 9th December 1915, this newly-created system started operating.[20]

The initial job of this body was to restore order by all conceivable means and to control the thirty-two tamasha mandali groups, consisting of about a hundred persons and also to organize a body with a regulated constitution. It was informed that Sai Baba had given his consent to Sathe to create and head such a body which was immediately formed under the name "Durbar Mandal". The Durbar Mandal connected itself with the executive (village) body and jointly created Dakshina Bhiksha Sanstha, Saiabad. The reason for the creation of D.B.S. was made clear to all the attendees. "The Dakshina-Bhiksha Sanstha, deriving its authority from Shree Sai Nath, through Mr. H.V. Sathe, thus established itself to act as His duly authorised deputy in all matters" (*Sainath Prabha* Kiran 2, 1916: 44).

The Sanstha decided:

> Firstly, to establish and maintain order in place of existing disorder and to provide comforts to Shree Sai Maharaj and His bhaktas, local and mofussil; secondly, to start and maintain charitable and instructional institutions, in harmony with Shree Baba's love for mankind; i.e. to erect Dharmashalas, Pathashalas, Annachatras, Rest-houses, Mutts, Devalayas, Ghats, Mandaps, Tanks, Wells &c., for the convenience of pilgrims, general visitors and the villagers; thirdly, to collect, compare, and compile Shree's Upadeshes, stories and other renderings, with His bhaktas' experiences, in book and pamphlet series, publishing them from time to time, with the main view of recording them, for the benefit of His bhaktas and the general public; fourthly, to establish the Dakshina-Bhiksha Sanstha as an appendage of Shree Sai Baba, to look after all worldly affairs of His, being in actual charge of or controlling all His present estate and others that might be added to it in future, and managing all the connected establishments of His Person and the Sanstha; fifthly, *to* scheme out and provide the Sanstha with necessary funds and estate by every conceivable method; and finally, to establish the Sanstha in a manner adequate to the growing interests and importance of Shirdi, Shree Sai Baba and His bhaktas.

Sainath Prabha Kiran 2, 1916: 44–45

There is a discussion about the mankaris and sevakaris and some others who used to get disbursement out of the dakshina money received by Sai Baba, mostly from the devotees coming from other places. Some of the sevakaris even made it difficult for the visiting devotees to have a clear or undisturbed darshan of Sai Baba. The sevakaris used their proximity and contact with Sai Baba to their own advantage, which the D.B.S. wanted to stop.

Accordingly, on 12th December, the Sanstha introduced the practice of donating seeda to the visiting devotees, calculated on need-based requirements. Sai Baba, in an open durbar, when approving the system of giving seeda, limited the donation of seeda to a person to three days only.[21]

In the meantime, Sathe invited P.J. Mead, the Collector of the district of Ahmednagar in whose jurisdiction Shirdi existed. In the presence of the villagers, Collector Mead, thanked the Sanstha for the invitation and expressed his pleasure for establishment of the Sanstha to regulate Sai Baba's affairs.[22] It was an important step taken by H.V. Sathe to involve the government machinery and get its indirect support for D.B.S.

For financial management, the D.B.S. introduced a bhiksha programme and a dakshina programme as Sai Baba and his poor and destitute bhaktas mostly depended on the earning from bhiksha and dakshina. That is why the body was named as Dakshina Bhiksha Sanstha. The Sanstha proposed that those who received money from Sai Baba should donate a certain percentage (say 10 per cent) of such income to the D.B.S. for fulfilling the daily needs of Sai Baba like food, tobacco and oil, etc.[23]

Till then, no record of the receipts pertaining to the bhiksha and dakshina donated to Sai Baba was maintained. An account statement, regarding the receipts and expenditure of bhiksha and dakshina was introduced by the D.B.S. Both Sathe and the Sanstha were of the view that money doled out by Sai Baba could be used for charity purposes, for example, creating lodging facilities for students. Hence, D.B.S. requested devotees to donate some money to the Sanstha.[24] Tatya Kote Patil, who joined the Sanstha, was chosen to be the Chairman of the Karyakari Mandal.[25] He promised to pay to the Sanstha one third of whatever money he received from Sai Baba during a month. Murabe Mehraban Pir Muhammad alias Bade Baba[26] used to take daily dakshina from Sai Baba and promised to pay one third of his earnings from Sai Baba to D.B.S.

However, Bade Baba, who had benefitted the most, never made any contribution, what to speak of other beneficiaries!

Thus, Mote Baba, alias, Fakir Baba, has been enjoying the discontinued bounties of the Trikalagyakaishwarya Shree Sainath, for nearly five years . . . receiving an estimated average figure amounting to at least half a lac rupees, since his arrival.

Sainath Prabha Kiran 2, 1916: 65–66[27]

In this context, a written statement by Tatya which was handed over to the D.B.S. on 25th December 1915, is relevant. It gives a clear picture about the happenings at Shirdi at that time. Tatya was a protégé of Sai Baba. He slept with Sai Baba for fourteen years in Dwarkamayi Masjid.[28] Hence, he cannot be expected to give false or exaggerated statement on matters pertaining to his spiritual Guru and mentor.

Tatya Kote Patil's written statement given to Shri Saiabad Sansthan in Marathi (photographs 7.1 a, b and c) is translated into English:

I am a resident of Shirdi. Shri Samarth Sai Baba has reared me from my very birth. My parents are also at his constant service. We consider him as our father and family deity and continue to do so till today. Approximately twelve years ago, Shri Sai never used to take any dakshina from anyone. He used to take bhiksha from some particular houses of the village for his living. During my childhood, my parents used to fulfil some of his needs. As I grew up, after my father's demise, I am fulfilling some of his needs. As the fame of Shri started spreading, the number of devotees visiting him started increasing. That is why I am now bearing the expenses as and when required. I serve him with the thought that I am his son. Every day, the expenditure is increasing. The daily expenditure has increased from Rs. 75 to Rs. 125. These expenses are being met through the dakshina received from the devotees of Shri and the difference, if any, is being met by me. My financial condition is much better now with Shri Baba's kripa and my landholdings have increased by hundred pattas. This is all due to the blessings of Shri Samarth's divine feet. . . . Since the last two years, due to his old age and detached behaviour, some unscrupulous and selfish villagers have started misbehaving with him. As Sai Baba gives me some money daily for meeting expenses, some people used to think that they can also take money from him fraudulently. On the pretext of bhakri, masalas, oil, tobacco, vegetables, they used to take money and the result was that evil characters, dancers, tamashawallas from different villages used to come, make the ladies dance at Dwarkamayi and take Rs. 2 per dance from Sai Baba. The villagers started taking their commission from this and this is how the dalali (commission) started in right earnest. This had a huge impact on Shri's health and peace and he was falling sick very often. Whenever I or other devotees used to go for his darshan, in anguish he would say "I have so many people, at least do some arrangements." . . . When nothing worked out, Sai Baba directed Bapusaheb Jog and Damu Anna Chinchnikar to send a message to Sathe and Chandorkar to come and make some arrangements. Shri Chandorkar could not come due to some reason but Sathe came immediately on 6.12.1915. On the next day, when Sathe was sitting in front of Shri Baba, Shri said *"Saheb, hey tu paahtos naa? Yaancha kaahin tari bandobast kara. Ugeech kaai baslaas?*

[Saheb, can you see this, do some arrangements for this, why are you sitting quietly.]

After understanding the purport of Sai Baba's orders, Sathe acted immediately.

This was told to Sathe in front of many people like Dr. Pillay and Sundar Narayan. Sathe immediately after going back called Anna Chinchnikar and Dr. Pillay and asked them what can be done in regard to Sai Baba's directives. On the behest of Dr. Sahib, Sundarrao Narayan and Keshav Raghunath Deshpande with my help formed a working group (Vyavasthapan mandal). A meeting was convened on 9th

December 1915 and villagers and devotees from other places were invited. They apportioned Sai Baba's work and gave responsibility to the people for making arrangements. Most important thing that happened was the ongoing dance and tamasha events came to an end. From that day, the system of managing Sai Baba's accounts started. On the next day, the groups were called and asked if they would be willing to submit an account of the donations received by them from Sai Baba on a daily basis. To this I answered that Sai Baba is my God and as I am close to him, I am responsible for this sort of management and shall give the statement of earnings and expenditure. Besides this, I shall also give the account of the money used to support many other people in the name of Shri. I will provide this information in 4-5 days and I am willing to help the groups in all possible ways.

> 25th Dec 1915, Tatya alias Ganpatrao Patil Kote)
> Witness: Ramchandra Dada Patil Kote
> Bayaji Appa Patil Kote
> Pandurang Bhikaji Patil Shelke
> Sakharam Mahadu Patil Kote

Sainath Prabha Kiran 1, 1916: 43–47, self-translated[29]

Tatya was reputed to be a straightforward person. This is the most authentic written statement made by one of the closest devotees of Sai Baba, in the presence of four prominent persons who were also devotees of Sai Baba. This written statement of Tatya is published in Sainath Prabha Kiran 1 Issue 1916. As mentioned in Tatya's statement, Sai Baba used to give vent to his uncomfortable feelings at times:

Malaa Pastava yeto, lokanala pahile tar; Meech ghokani karto.

Sainath Prabha Kiran 2, 1916: 74

[When I see people behaving in this manner, I do repent and I go on thinking about it.]

The initial actions of the D.B.S. to control the unruly persons at Shirdi yielded some results. The nuisance of the tamashawallas was contained and a more conducive atmosphere was created to carry on with religious pursuits. The Ramnavami festival was celebrated in a better manner in 1916 due to the active support rendered by the D.B.S.

किरण १ ळें.   ५७

परिशिष्ट (अ).

(कलम २) मध्यें उल्लेखिलेलें.)

श्री.

दिवाणबहादूर श्रीसाई–आबाद् संस्थान, यांचे समोर:–
मी तात्या बिन गणपतराव कोते, पाटील, राहणार
शिर्डी, विचारल्यावरून माहिती लिहून देतों कीं:—

"मी शिर्डी येथील राहणारा असोन, माझे जन्मापासून
माझा सर्व प्रकारें सांभाळ श्रीसमर्थ साईबाबांनींच केला
आहे. माझे आईबापहि श्रीसमर्थांचे नेहमीं सेवेंत असून,
त्मर्थ आमचे घरांतील वडील व आमचें कुळ–दैवत, असें
समजून त्याप्रमाणें आम्हीं आजपर्यंत चालत आलों आहों.
सुमारें बारा वर्षांपूर्वींपर्यंत श्रीसमर्थ कोणाकडूनहि दक्षिणा
वगैरे कांहीं घेत नसत. त्यांचा उदर–निर्वाह गांवांत घरो-
विद्ध घरीं भिक्षा–भाकरीच्या–मागून ते करीत असत. प्रसंगीं
कांहीं बाबतींत जरूर लागल्यास–मी लहान होतों तोंपर्यंत–
माझे आईबाप पुरवठा करीत असत. मी वयांत आल्या-
पासून वडिलांचे पश्चात् मी करीत आहें. पुढें दिवसेंदिवस
श्रींचे तप जसजसें वाढत गेलें, तसतसें भक्त लोक फार
येऊं लागले. आणि त्याकरितां ज्या ज्या वेळीं अवश्य लागणारे
सर्च ते मी करीत आलों. व हे सर्व सर्च मी श्रीसमर्थांचा
मुलगा आहें असें समजून केले आहेत. पुढें दिवसें-
दिवस सर्च वाढत चाललां. तो आतांपर्यंत दररोज सुमारें
धये ७५ पासून १२५ पर्यंत वाढला आहे. हा सर्व सर्च,
श्रींना भक्तमंडळीकडून मिळणारी दक्षिणा–व कमजास्ती
रागल्यास माझे स्वतःचे इष्टेटींतुन, याप्रमाणें भागवीत आहों.

c

Photograph 7.1a: Statement of Tatya Ganpati Kote Patil given to Shri Saiabad Sansthan

मी पूर्वी ज्या स्थितींत होतों, ती श्रीबाबांचे कृपेनें हल्लीं १०० पटींहून जास्त सौख्याची झालेली असोन, हें सर्व श्रेय श्रीसमर्थांचे चरणांचें आहे, ही गोष्ट मी स्वतः कबुल करितोंच आहें. परंतु गांवांतील सर्व मंडळीसहि आणि इतर ठिकाणचे श्रींचे भक्तमंडळीसहि माहित आहे. श्रीबाबांचे भक्तांसरीज इतर मंडळीस याबद्दल कांहीं भ्रांति असल्यास ती समर्थच दूर करणार आहेत.

अलीकडे गेल्या दोन वर्षांपासून श्रींचे वृद्धपणामुळें आणि त्यांचे विरक्तपणानें गांवांतील कांहीं असमंजस व स्वार्थी लोकांस श्रींचे महत्व न समजून त्यांनीं बरेंच अनाचाराचें वगैरे वर्तन सुरु केलें; आणि मला ज्याप्रमाणें सर्चाकरितां श्री दररोज कांहीं रकम देतात त्याचप्रमाणें लोकांनीं वाटेल तसा बहाणा करून, श्रीस सतावून, कांहीं तरी कारणानिमित्त—मला सर्चाकरितां देत असत त्याप्रमाणें आपणहि उपटूं लागले. कोणी, माकरीकरितां, सर्पणाकरितां, मडाल्याकरितां, तेलाकरितां, तंबाखू, माजीपाला, अशा निरनिराळ्या सबबींनें, पैसे घेतां घेतां असेंर त्याचा परिणाम गांवोगांवचे तमाशेवाले लोक आणवून, मशिदींत दुराचारी स्त्रियांचे नाचतमाशे सुरु करून, त्यांना श्रीकडून दररोज प्रत्येक नाचणारणीस दोन रुपयेप्रमाणें देण्यास लावून, त्यांपैकीं त्यांचे पोटापुरते पैसे त्यांस देऊन, बाकी रुपये आपण उपटावे; असा दलालीचा धंदा सुरु झाला. आणि या कारणामुळें श्रीसमर्थांना—स्वतःचे शरीरास, त्यांचे तपास, आणि त्यांचे मनास,—इतका त्रास झाला कीं, समर्थ वेळोवेळीं शरीरानें अतिशय आजारी होऊं लागले. आणि

आम्ही अगर इतर भक्तमंडळी ज्या ज्या वेळीं त्यांचे दर्शनास जाऊं त्या त्या वेळीं त्यांनी असे उद्गार निघूं लागले कीं:—'अरे ! माझीं इतकीं माणसें आहेत, कोणी तरी बंदोबस्त करा" असें म्हणूं लागले. परंतु हे सर्व अनाचार-श्रीपुढें होत असलेले-ते स्वतः पाहून, स्वस्थ बसून,—त्यांचे विलक्षण सामर्थ्य हे सर्व अनाचार बंद करण्याचें असतां तसें न करितां—' कोणी तरी बंदोबस्त करारे ! ' असें म्हणतात. यामुळें ह्यांचे सर्व रहस्य काय आहे हें कोणासहि समजेना ! शेवटीं डिसेंबर तारीख १ च्या सुमारास श्रीचे वृद्ध भक्तांपैकीं दामुअण्णा चिन्चणीकर व दापुसोहेब जोग या दोघांस श्रींनीं असें सांगितलें कीं:—"रा. रा. नारायण गोविंद उर्फ नानासाहेब चांदोरकर अथवा रावबहाद्दूर हरि विनायक उर्फ तात्या साहेब साठे या दोघांस पत्र पाठवून तावडतोब बोलावून आणा; म्हणजे ते माझा बंदोबस्त करितील." यावरून वरील उभयतां भक्तांस पत्रें लिहिण्यांत आलीं. पैकी नानासाहेब चांदोरकर यांस कांहीं अडचणीमुळें येतां आलें नाहीं. रावबहाद्दूर साठे साहेबांनीं तावडतोब येऊन, तां० ६।१२।१५ रोजीं श्रींचें दर्शन घेतलें. दुसरे दिवशीं सकाळीं समर्थांसन्निध बसले असतां, श्रीबाबा म्हणालें:—"साहेब ! हें तूं पाहतोस ना ! याचा कांहीं तरी बंदोबस्त कर. उगिच काय बसलास ?" ही गोष्ट पुष्कळ मंडळी, त्यांत मुख्यत्वेंकरून डॉक्टर पिले व सुंदरराव नारायण यांचे समक्ष सांगितली. साठे साहेबांनीं तावडतोब घरी येऊन, रा. अण्णा चिन्चणीकर व डॉक्टर पिले यांस बोलावून "श्रीचे आज्ञेसंबंधानें काय तजवीज करावी" असा पत्र केला. त्यावर डॉ० साहेब यांचे सूचनेवरून सुंदरराव

Photograph 7.1b: Statement of Tatya Ganpati Kote Patil given to Shri Saiabad Sansthan.

साईनाथ-प्रभा.

नारायण व केशवराव रघुनाथ देशपांडे यांस आपले साह्यास घेऊन, एक व्यवस्थापक मंडळ स्थापन करण्याचें ठरलें. आणि झाप्रमाणें योजना ठागठीच अंमलांत आणून, गांवांतील व इतर ठिकाणची भक्तमंडळींची सभा ता॰ ९।१२।१५ रोजीं बोलाविली; व श्रींच्या कामासंबं- धानें विभागणी करून, प्रत्येक कामासंबंधानें गांवांतील ठोकांची सभा नेमून तिच्याकडेच झ्याची व्यवस्था सोप- विली. आणि हें झाल्यावरोबर प्रथम अतिशय महत्वाची कामगिरी म्हणजे याच दिवशीं तमाशे बंद आले ! आणि त्याच दिवशीं श्रींचे सर्चासंबंधानें हिशोब ठेवण्यास सुरवात झाली. दुसरे दिवशीं मंडळींकडून मठा बोलावणें झालें, व असें विचारलें कीं " तुम्ही श्रीबाबांकडून जे पैसे घेतां,- म्हणजे बाबा तुम्हांस-दररोज सायंकाळीं देतात,- त्यांचा हिशोब तुम्हीं देऊं शकाल काय ? " स्याकरून मीं उत्तर दिलें कीं-"आपण आतां विचारतां या गोष्टी- संबंधानें असा कोणीतरी विचारणारा श्रींचेसंबंधानें असावा, आणि तें सांगतील त्या धोरणानें आमचे हातून सर्व प्रकारें व्यवस्था व्हावी, हें मला इष्ट आहे. आणि याकरितां माझी अशी कबुली आहे, कीं, श्रीकडून दररोज जे पैसे मठा देण्यांत येत आहेत, ते मी आजपासून मंडळींकडे देण्यास तयार आहें. " आणि याचप्रमाणें श्रींचे पैशाचा हिशोब मंडळींकडे देण्यास सुरवात करून उठतेवेळीं मी त्यास विनंति केली कीं– "श्रींजवळ माझा निकटसंबंध असल्या- मुळें आणि त्यांची योग्यप्रकारें व्यवस्था लागावी यासाठीं, त्यांचे पैशासंबंधाचे इतर जे व्यवहार हल्लीं आहेत, त्याची मला असढेली माहिती मंडळींस मी मोठ्या खुषीनें देईन.

किरण १ ळें.

द्विःयेक मंडळींस पैशासंबंधीज इतर प्रकारचीहि मदत श्रींचे नांवासाठीं होत आहे. आणि याजबद्दलची पूर्ण माहिती चौकशी करून मंडळींकडे कळवीन; ही माहिती ५।५ दिव- सांत कळवीन आणि हरएक प्रकारची-मांसकडून होणारी- मदत करण्यास मी तयार आहें; हें लिहून दिलें. ता॰ २५ माहे डिसेंबर सन १९१५. इ.

१ सही तात्या बिन गण्पतराव पाटील कोते
दस्तुर खुद.

साक्ष.

१ रामचंद्र दादा पाटील कोते दस्तुर खुद.
१ धयाजी आपाजी पाटील कोते द॰ खु॰
१ सही पांडुरंग भिकाजी पाटील शेळके द॰ खु॰
१ सखाराम महादू पाटील कोते द॰ खु॰

Photograph 7.1c: Statement of Tatya Ganpati Kote Patil given to Shri Saiabad Sansthan

Regulating Financial Dealings: Resistance from Vested Interests

However, problems arose when the newly created Sanstha tried to regulate the financial dealings which included receipt and disbursement of the dakshina money received by Sai Baba on a daily basis and taking a contribution from it for use of the Sanstha. A large group of people who did not want to abide by such a regulation, questioned the right of the Sanstha to collect such money. Sathe tried to convince them by saying that the best way to repay the divine grace of the guru is to donate some money to the D.B.S. which can be utilized for his food and other needs. These people did not accept that Sathe had Sai Baba's consent and the authority to control things at Shirdi, including such financial matters. They asserted their direct relationship with Sai Baba as per the guru-shishya tradition. They shunned an intermediary like Sathe or a Dakshina Bhiksha Sanstha between them and Sai Baba. Mr. Chitambar Keshav Gadgil, pensioned Mamlatdar, had all the accounts and papers of the Sanstha but unfortunately, he died in December 1917[30] without handing them over to the Sanstha. When Sathe asked Sai Baba about his suggestions of the continuance of the Sanstha, Sai Baba said, "The Sanstha must continue. It shall not be broken by anybody" (*Sainath Prabha* Kiran 5, 1918: 2). On the other hand, Sathe and his group were convinced that some people around Sai Baba were misleading him and therefore,

> Justice demands the execution of such an urgent reform. Society requires better manners and more so, the bhavic and wholesome surroundings of Shree Sai Baba.

> *Sainath Prabha* Kiran 2, 1916: 93

From December 1915 till the end of 1916, the D.B.S., in spite of opposition from certain quarters, sustained itself. It brought out a bilingual magazine in English and

Marathi titled *Sainath Prabha* from April 1916 to propagate the deeds and philosophy of Sai Baba and the happenings around him.

Unfortunately, an incident took place towards the end of 1916 that created a cleavage between the core workers of the Durbar Mandal of D.B.S. One lady devotee of Sai Baba, by the name of Radhakrishna Ayi, passed away in November 1916. This devotee had collected a lot of costly and decorative items, bordering on regality, for the use of Sai Baba, particularly in the Dwarkamayi–Chawadi procession. These included the palki, chhatar, morcha, chamar, etc. After her demise, there was a question about the custody of this property. The police of Rahata took the immediate charge of the property and later handed the items over to Sathe.

In November 1916 Radha-krishnabai a devotee of Sainath died. . . . As a natural sequence government intervened and all the articles found in Radha-krishnabai's custody at the police inquiry were handed over to Raobahadur H.V. Sathe, the president of the Sanstha. . . . Hence forward this became the bone of contention among the several members of the Sanstha. The work was hampered and the progress came to a standstill.

Sainath Prabha Kiran 5, 1918: 1

After the body of Radha Krishna was sent away for Post Mortem the Police from Rahata, were busy for 2 or 3 days, making an inventory of all the properties of Shree Sai Baba, that were in the Koti in her custody, which they left in temporary charge of Messrs. Sakharam Hari Jog and Thatya [Tatya] Ganpatrao Patel Kothe. In this connection, it must be said, that the Police officers, at first, consulted the wishes of the Dakshina Bhiksha Sanstha, to accept the custody of Shree Sai Baba's property; but, when the latter, for their own reasons, declined to accept the offer, with thanks, the arrangement as stated above was done. Some two months afterwards in accordance with an order received from the higher authorities, the Fouzdar of Rahata again handed over custody of the listed articles to the Dakshina Bhiksha Santha, about the first week of February last.

Sainath Prabha Kiran 4, 1917: 129

This change of custodial rights from the hands of Bapusaheb Jog and Tatya to the hands of Dakshina Bhiksha Sanstha precipitated a division among them.

Bapusaheb Jog and Tatya Kote Patil and some others were on one side and H.V. Sathe and D.B.S. on the other side.

Another incident accentuated the problems for Sathe. One of the devotees of Sai Baba named Shankar Narayan Vaidhya (or Joshi) alias Nanavali or Nana Buva, who was of queer and aggressive nature, threatened the Naib Diwan of D.B.S. and Sathe. Sathe was advised by his father-in-law Dada Kelkar and some well-wishers to immediately leave Shirdi to avoid a mishap (*Sainath Prabha* Kiran 4, 1917: 142–143).[31]

Heeding their advice, Sathe left Shirdi in 1917 to return after Sai Baba's Mahasamadhi in 1918. Nanavali is reported to have left his body on the thirteenth day from Sai Baba's Mahasamadhi in October 1918. The absence of Sathe from Shirdi under such conditions was one of the reasons why the D.B.S. could not consolidate its position and gradually lost ground.

Unfortunately, before the scheme of Shri Saibaba Sansthan could be fully implemented, Sai Baba passed away on 15th October 1918 and his body was entombed in Buti wada. This changed the scenario. Although for some time the worship of Sai Baba continued at his Samadhi located inside the Buti wada, the need for another organizational management system was urgently felt.

Formation of Shri Sainath Sansthan Committee: Smooth Transition through Amalgamation of D.B.S.

The educated and responsible devotees of Sai Baba like Kakasaheb Dixit, Gopalrao Buti and many others felt that an organizational management system was urgently needed. Hence, they joined together and formed the Shri Sainath Sansthan Committee (S.S.S.C.) in order to create a proper organization to take care of Sai Baba's affairs after his Mahasamadhi. On 22nd October 1918, an application was made to the Collector and District Magistrate of Ahmednagar by Hari Sitaram Dixit, solicitor on behalf of S.S.S.C. The petition stated that the Sansthan was formed after Sai Baba of Shirdi breathed his last on Tuesday, 15th October 1918, with the intention to manage his shrine and his property. The various articles used for worship of Sai Baba, articles of processional paraphernalia including the horse, palanquin, rath as well as the articles personally used by Sai Baba, which were to be preserved for their sanctity and worship by devotees and other sundry articles like cooking pots, etc., had already been taken over by the Mamlatdar of Kopargaon.

In the petition, dated 22nd October 1918, the Collector and District Magistrate of Ahmednagar was requested to issue orders to deliver the entire property to the president of Shri Sainath Sansthan Committee, i.e., Gopalrao Mukund Buti alias Bapusaheb Buti. The application was signed by Hari Sitaram Dixit and endorsed by Hari Vinayak Sathe. Thus, there was a healthy involvement of two different organizations by the names of S.S.S.C. (under the presidentship of G.M. Buti) and D.B.S. (under the presidentship of H.V. Sathe) and they were amalgamated[32] (*Sainath Prabha* Kiran 11, 1918: 16–18; Annexure-1).

Accordingly, the entire property was handed over to Buti, functioning in the capacity of the president of S.S.S.C. The support of Sathe was an important factor in the smooth settlement of the issue about the custodianship of the property.

> As the shrine will be a permanent institution it was deemed necessary to have a body to manage the same and the undermentioned persons were accordingly constituted into a Committee for the purpose of managing the said institution, under the name of Shri Sainath Sansthan Committee and the Dakshina Bhiksha Sanstha has been amalgamated with it.
>
> *Sainath Prabha* Kiran 11, 1918: 17

Thus, we cannot say that the D.B.S. created by H.V. Sathe was a failure. Sathe was a great devotee of Sai Baba who tried to do his best when ordered by Sai Baba. To him goes the credit of building the first wada at Shirdi at Sai Baba's behest and also to publish the first exclusive magazine titled *Sainath Prabha* dedicated to Sai Baba. He tried to institutionalize the various activities (including that of finance) around Sai Baba at Shirdi by establishing the D.B.S.

For some time, this Sanstha tried to manage Sai Baba's affairs in an organized manner. Sathe, being a retired Deputy Collector in the British government, had the wherewithal and experience to create and manage D.B.S. effectively. No other person could have dared to undertake such a difficult task under the prevailing circumstances of Shirdi. Sai Baba had full confidence in Sathe and therefore, he had invited him to undertake the job.

The D.B.S. and *Sainath Prabha* can be said to be the precursors of Shri Saibaba Sansthan Trust and *Shri Sai Leela* magazine that came to existence in 1922 and 1923 respectively, thereby marking their great importance and contribution.

******

Notes

1. "The houses on his daily begging round included those of two wealthy land owners namely Waman Gondkar Patil and Wamen Sakharam Shelke. Another house belong[ed] to Bayajabai Kote, a lady devotee who had formally fed him in the forest. The fourth house belonged to Bayyaji Appa Kote Patil, who became a sevakari (personal attendant) of the saint. The fifth and the last house belonged to a local money lender, Nandaram Marwari" (Shepherd 2017: 61).

   Five houses namely of Bayajabai Kote Patil, Radhabai Gondkar Patil, Santaji Bhivsan Shelke Patil, Nandram Shet Marwari, Appaji Kote Patil (Kavade 1956: 35).

2. Dabholkar (1930: 101).

3. Swami (1994b: 113); *Shri Sai Leela* (Issue 1, 1923: 16).

4. Few known personalities of that time like: G.S. Khaparde, Advocate of Amravati; M.B. Rege, judge of High Court Indore; Kakasaheb Dixit, Solicitor of Bombay; G.G. Narke, Professor, Geology & Chemistry, College of Engineering Deccan Gymkhana, Poona; Nanasaheb Chandorkar, Deputy Collector; P.R. Avastey, judge of Gwalior; M.W. Pradhan, Member Legislative Council; B.V. Dev, Retired first class magistrate, Thane.

5. Dabholkar (1930: 637).

6. Swami (1994a: 37).

7. Changes in the nature of worship were:
   a. "The next step was from individual worship to congregational worship. It was in 1908 that the change had started" (Swami 1994a: 36–37).
   b. "Only in 1910 did there commence what some commentators refer to as 'Congregational worship'" (Shepherd 2015: 138).
   c. "From 10 Dec 1909 devotees began to offer regular worship to Baba in the Chavadi" (Gunaji 2002: 197).

8. *Shri Sai Leela* (1923: 17).

9. *Sainath Prabha* (Kiran 1, 1916: 11); Ibid (Kiran 2, 1916: 46).

10. "When Sri Sai Baba came to Shirdi in the mid–nineteenth century, it was a rustic hamlet of about a thousand people (mostly labourers & artisans), with approx. . . 200 houses" (Williams 2002: 1).

    In 1910 Shirdi had about 400 mud-brick houses, big and small, existing in narrow lanes. . . . The population was approx . . . 2,500" (Shepherd 2015: 4).

11. "Shirdi is a small village of about 1,500 living souls, of both sexes, young and old" (*Sainath Prabha* Kiran 1, 1916: 2 (I)).

    "Fleeting time of about fifteen years of Shree Sai Munivarya's rising in Shirdi, has worked out, of an insignificant, plain, village of but fifteen hundred souls, crouching under their humble, mud enclosures of so-called houses" (Ibid: 22).

12. *Sainath Prabha* (Kiran 1, 1916: 14–28) gives a detailed view of "How unpleasant societies and their troubles developed."

13. Swami (1994: 35, 38, 70).

14. Dabholkar (1930: 782–783).

15. "His gifts are frequent and unprecedented in extent. His care for the poor, the needy and the crippled, He exhibits by special charities at fixed hours daily" (*Sainath Prabha* Kiran 1, 1916: 21).

16. Ibid (Kiran 2, 1916: 35).

17. Ibid: 33.

18. Ibid: 36.

19. *Sainath Prabha* (Kiran 2, 1916: 41–42).

20. Ibid: 42.

21. Ibid: 49.

22. Ibid: 50.

23. Ibid: 52–53.

24. Ibid: 52–54.

25. Ibid: 62–63.

26. Ibid: 63.

27. "Bade Baba who got plenty of money and paid income tax on them subsequently lost all fortune and died" (Swami 1941: 85).

28. Dabholkar (1930: 149).

29. *Sainath Prabha* (Kiran 1, 1916: 43–47).

30. *Sainath Prabha* (Kiran 5, 1918: 2).

31. "In the durbar of Sri Sai Baba and when he issued out in solemn pomp, I carried the mace before him. Many were jealous of me because of the distinction I enjoyed. These and the villagers leagued together and used Nana Wali to molest me and drive me away from Shirdi. Once I was carrying the mace before Baba, Nana Wali came up and scratched the back of my head with the sharp point of broken glass. In self-defence, I had to seize him and press him down on a pile of logs lying on the roadside. Sai Baba cried out "Saheb, do not do so." . . . One day, as I intended to go to the Mosque to offer Naivedya to Baba very early (as I had to proceed on a particular trip) my Father-in-law rushed in and adjured me to desist from going to the Mosque, as Nana Wali was standing at the entrance, hatchet in hand, with deadly intention and as he would make short work of me. So without taking any leave, I went away and left Shirdi for good" (Swami 2006: 117).

"H.V. Sathe was once asked how he continued to believe in Baba, even though Baba could not save him from the mischief of Nana Wali. Sathe replied, 'Just as the Minister of the Peshwa was murdered right in front of Vittal at Pandharpur. That did not however prevent people from believing in Vittal even though Vittal did not save him.' Similarly his own faith in Sai Baba was unaffected by Nana Wali's threats" (Swami 1994c: 115).

32. *Sainath Prabha* (Kiran 11, 1918: 16–18).

8

Sainath Prabha: (1916–1919)

(The First Journal Published during Shri Sai Baba's Time)

This chapter outlines the origin and contribution of Sainath Prabha, the first bilingual magazine on Shri Sai Baba (1916–1919).

Most of the people connected with Sai Baba of Shirdi as devotees, writers or research scholars, are generally aware about the magazine *Shri Sai Leela* which is being published since 1923 by Shirdi Sansthan, now known as Shri Saibaba Sansthan Trust, Shirdi, Maharashtra, as its official publication. Later, in 1930, the Sansthan published *Shri Sai Satcharita*, an anthology on Sai Baba, written by Govind Raghunath Dabholkar alias Hemadpant.[1]

Prior to the publication of *Shri Sai Leela*, the only other way in which people could learn about Sai Baba was through the kathakars like Dasganu. He used to perform kirtans in religious gatherings and functions and narrate about the greatness, generosity and miracles of Sai Baba in great detail. Before the publication of *Sai Satcharita* (1930) and *Shri Sai Leela* (1923), only a few booklets and small compendiums were available on the saints of Maharashtra, including Sai Baba, written mostly in Marathi.[2]

However, it is not widely known that a printed magazine, captioned *Sainath Prabha*, was published for the first time in April 1916 from Shirdi, when Sai Baba was in his human embodiment. This bilingual magazine in English and Marathi, was printed at Pune, Maharashtra. There is only a brief mention about *Sainath Prabha* in some books[3] (photograph 8.1).

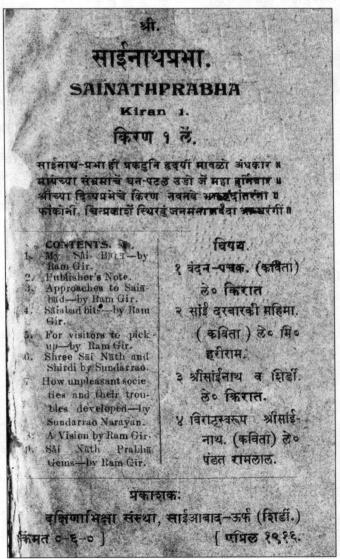

Photograph 8.1: Cover page of *Sainath Prabha* Kiran 1, 1916

Govind Raghunath Dabholkar mentions:

> Some nos. of *Sai Nath Prabha*, a magazine published by
> Dakshina Bhiksha Sanstha, are also published.

Gunaji 2002: 6

Whereas Indira Kher says:

> Some eminent Sai devotees have published from Pune, a
> collection of Baba's stories, under the name *Sai Prabha*.

Kher 2016:19

This magazine was published by Sundarrao Narayan,
Naib Diwan, for the Dakshina Bhiksha Sanstha, Saiabad or
Shirdi Tal. Kopargoan Dist. Ahmednagar at 541 Budhwar
Peth, Poona City and was printed at the Aryabhushan Press,
Poona City by Anant Vinayak Patwardhan.[4] Following his
interview with Rao Bahadur H.V. Sathe, B.V. Narasimha
Swami confirms that an organization called Dakshina
Bhiksha Sanstha (D.B.S.) was set up and also that this
Sanstha published a journal called *Sainath Prabha*.[5]

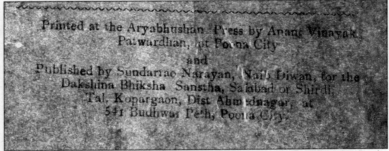

Photograph 8.2: Back page of *Sainath Prabha*, 1916

Besides such short remarks on D.B.S., most of the
writers have not even mentioned the name of this magazine
or that of D.B.S. in their books. It seems that access to this
rare document was not easy.[6]

In this magazine, Sai Baba has been addressed with unique epithets as Sai Prabhu (Sai as Lord), Muktidata (Liberator) and Shiladisha (The King of Shiladhi, now known as Shirdi) and also Sesha Sai and Renga Sai. Shirdi has been mentioned as "Mukti kshetra of the yuga" (place of liberation in this age) and also as Saiabad.[7]

This journal contains a lot of material to inform the readers, devotees and researchers about the religious, philanthropic, literary and social activities that happened during the presence of Sai Baba in Shirdi, from December 1916 onwards till his Mahasamadhi.

It seems that by 1918, Dabholkar, had collected a lot of anecdotes and other information regarding Sai Baba's personality, miracles, divine attributes, spiritual philosophy, relationship with the devotees and lifestyle from many sources which included the statements of the residents of Shirdi and the devotees visiting Sai Baba from other places. Dabholkar could write *Sai Satcharita* because he benefited from his direct communication with and proximity to Sai Baba and his devotees. He also witnessed many happenings around Sai Baba for a period of about eight years, between 1910 and 1918.[8] As advised by Sai Baba himself, he collected a lot of information, including anecdotes and also maintained a record, in order to write on the life of Sai Baba.[9]

In fact, Sai Baba had once, much earlier, addressed Dabholkar as "Hemadpant", predicting the creation of a valuable book like *Shri Sai Satcharita*. This book brought immense popularity to Dabholkar.[10]

An examination of the contents of *Sainath Prabha* reveals a lot of the anecdotes and information about that time at Shirdi. This is so because Rao Bahadur H.V. Sathe, the creator of this magazine, first came to Shirdi in April 1904 and visited Shirdi frequently after that to meet Sai Baba.[11] He was one of the closest devotees of Sai Baba and had a lot of interaction with him on numerous issues. Sai Baba used to rely on him a lot and fondly called him

"Saheb".[12] Sathe built the Sathe wada following the orders of Sai Baba. Sathe wrote a few articles under the caption "Sai Katha Karandak" and also edited the articles received from various writers for this magazine. Before he started writing articles in *Sainath Prabha* and editing the articles of others, he had been with Sai Baba for twelve years.

Some educated persons of that time used to maintain personal diaries e.g., Ganesh Shrikrishna Khaparde, Kakasaheb Dixit and a few others.[13] When in Shirdi, some of them used to make notes about the happenings around Sai Baba and also about their experience with him. The original diary of Kakasaheb Dixit is lost, but a copy of some portions of the diary is available. The authenticity of this diary and its contents were verified from Anil Dixit, the grandson of Kakasaheb Dixit and son of Ramkrishna Hari Dixit (fondly called "Babu" by Sai Baba).

Establishment of Dakshina Bhiksha Sanstha and Publication of Sainath Prabha

The circumstances under which Dakshina Bhiksha Sanstha was created were discussed in chapter 7 and also the publication of *Sainath Prabha* magazine. As the fame of Sai Baba spread, there was a massive increase in the flow of urban and rural visitors to Shirdi, especially from the year 1908 onwards. The serene atmosphere of Shirdi was replaced by a lot of hustle-bustle. Soon, a group of motivated individuals started indulging in various types of undesirable activities that disturbed the peace around Sai Baba. Frequent quarrels in place of pothi parayana and kirtans, manipulation of naivedya items from Sai Baba by pushing the children to the front, extortion of money systematically on different pretexts and display of impertinent behaviour, even in the presence of Sai Baba, pervaded the atmosphere.[14] Even Sai Baba was greatly concerned about the prevailing situation.

Hence, Sai Baba wanted Rao Bahadur H.V. Sathe, a resident of Poona and Narayan Govind Chandorkar to come to Shirdi immediately and make appropriate arrangements to establish order.

On receiving intimation, Sathe rushed to Shirdi on Friday, 3rd December 1915.[15]

Being a retired Deputy Collector, Sathe had the required skill-set to solve the problems. First, he formed the D.B.S. under the aegis of which he began the publication of *Sainath Prabha* to propagate the holy name and pious deeds of Sai Baba and happenings around Sai Baba in Shirdi.

The list of issues of *Sainath Prabha* that were published can be seen in table 8.1.

Table 8.1: Sainath Prabha: April 1916 to October 1919

SAINATH PRABHA		SAINATH PRABHA	
KIRAN	Edition	KIRAN	Edition
Kiran 1	April 1916	Kiran 1 (Varsh 2)	January 1919
Kiran 2	September 1916	Kiran 2	February 1919
Kiran 3	February 1917	Kiran 3	March 1919
Kiran 4	May 1917	Kiran 4	Apr 1919
The magazine stopped for 1 year		Kiran 5	May 1919
Kiran 5 (Varsh 1)	May 1918	Kiran 6	June 1919
Kiran 6	June 1918	Kiran 7	July 1919
Kiran 7	July 1918	Kiran 8	August 1919
Kiran 8	August 1918	Kiran 9-10	September/ October 1919
Kiran 9	September 1918		
Kiran 10	October 1918		
Kiran 11	November 1918		
Kiran 12	December 1918		

Sainath Prabha: Form and Contents

Since, it is not possible to review all the issues of this magazine in this book, the contents of the first issue have primarily been mentioned here.

The first issue of *Sainath Prabha* was published in April 1916, about four months after the decision to publish the magazine was taken in December 1915 by the D.B.S. The magazine was dedicated to propagate the philosophy, pious deeds and anecdotes pertaining to Sai Baba. It also published news items on the happenings in Shirdi around Sai Baba.

The cover page of the April 1916 issue presents it as a bilingual magazine. It contains nine articles in English and four in Marathi. It says that D.B.S., located at Saiabad alias Shirdi, is the publisher. The back cover of the magazine declares the name of the printer as Anant Vinayak Patwardhan. This magazine was printed at the Aryabhushan Press, Poona city. Below these descriptions, there is a mention which reads: "Published by Sundarrao Narayan, Naib Diwan, for the Dakshina Bhiksha Sanstha, Saiabad or Shirdi, Tal. [Taluka] Kopargaon, Dist. Ahmednagar, at 541, Budhwar Peth, Poona city". In this issue, the nine articles written in English are in 112 pages and the four Marathi articles are in 24 pages. The issue is priced at six annas and the same price continues for the next issues also.[16] The advance annual subscription, priced at ₹3, is mentioned from the year 1918.[17]

In this issue, no name has been mentioned under the editor's or the publisher's note. Only "The Dakshina Bhiksha Sanstha" finds a mention. Six out of the nine articles contained in English are written by "Ram Gir" and two by "Sundarrao Narayan". In the Marathi section, two of the four articles are written by a writer named "Kirat" and one each by "Pandit Ram Lal" and "Hari Ram". The address of the writers is not mentioned.[18]

The front inner cover page has a beautiful poem about Sai Baba by Ram Gir followed by the publisher's note.

My Sai Baba

I went, I saw Shree Baba's
face, At Shirdi, a funny place,
None else I'd seen with face so bright,
With men around whose ways were light,
A father sure, a mother pure,
Would n'er have cured as He does lure,
A brother with love so dear,
On earth n'er came a fact to hear,
A Prince He is, a plain Fakir,
A Lord of course with no Fikir,
Distressed poor souls with love to cure,
Has come on earth, His ways are pure
A place to sit, a place to sleep,
All o'er He goes where men do weep,
With Karmic cares immersed so deep,
And lulls them all with just a sweep
To see His face men walk miles long,
Whatever creed they might belong,
Tan, Man and Dhan they freely give,
Such powers He wields, Him they believe
Their worries no more, their homes forgot,
With Him they stay, with bhav begot,
Full nights and days they pass away,
Ere they could see, they run away.
Hard days are lost, dark nights are bright,
With light divine, they run so light,
To all the poor men all alike,
His love is there and Him they like.

Ram Gir

Page 3 (i and ii) contains a ready reckoner for the devotees to reach Shirdi by rail. The last two paragraphs spell out the charter of D.B.S. Thereafter, the daily routine of Sai Baba is mentioned under the caption "Saiabad Bits" followed by general information for the benefit of the visitors coming to Shirdi.[19] Thus, the D.B.S., with the help of *Sainath Prabha* entered the public domain with the declaration that it could help the visiting devotees with boarding, lodging and darshan facilities at Shirdi and provide them with sanitary conveniences. For some time it's presence was felt in Shirdi, and people benefitted from the facilities provided by the D.B.S.

The paper and printing of the magazine are of high quality when compared to other books and magazines published at that time. The design and the contents of the magazine can be said to be good, keeping in mind that it was a new venture. Chapter II ends with a write-up captioned "Vision" by Ram Gir. The back cover contains an appeal to the devotees by the chitnis (secretary) of Dakshina Bhiksha Sanstha. The appeal is in Marathi (photograph 8.3) and has been translated into English in the notes at the end of this chapter.[20]

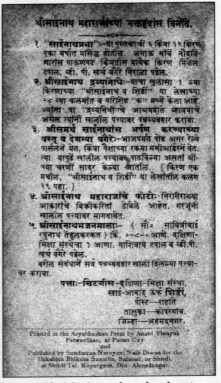

Photograph 8.3: Appeal to the devotees of Sai Maharaj

The second issue (Kiran 2) of *Sainath Prabha* was published in September 1916. The English section of this issue, contains nine articles in eighty-four pages besides the front page, an English poem on the inner side of the front page by Ram Gir, a publisher's note and an appeal to devotees.[21] The Marathi section consists of four articles and is of twenty-four pages, with some appendages.

Sathe in his interview to Narasimha Swami states that Ram Gir was none other than Sundarrao Narayan.

> I do not know what has become of Mr. Sunder Rao Narayan who was the editor and soul of "Sai Nath Prabha". It is he who signs his "apothegms" and his "vision" in Part I under the nom de plume "Ramagir".

> Swami 2006: 125

D.B.S. began to control and thus save the money doled out by Sai Baba to some unscrupulous devotees and the thirty-two tamashawallas.[22] The Sanstha tried to properly utilize the dakshina received by Sai Baba and created hindrances for the devotees who used to extract it from Sai Baba through devious means. It started functioning as a self-proclaimed authoritative organization on behalf of Sai Baba, which the crafty beneficiaries of Sai Baba's kindness could not tolerate.

As discussed in chapter 7, another controversy arose on the issue of the custody of the property of Sai Baba that Radhakrishna Ayi held in her personal custody before her demise in November 1916.[23]

The property became a bone of contention between H.V. Sathe and his group on one side and Tatya Kote Patil, Bapusaheb Jog and others on the other. Earlier, Tatya and Bapusaheb Jog used to support Dakshina Bhiksha Sanstha and Tatya was even an office-bearer of the Sanstha. As a consequence, the publication of the *Sainath Prabha* magazine and the contents of a few articles published in it were resented by the opposing group. The language of some of the articles was direct and offensive. Hence, a group of people, including Tatya, wanted the Sanstha to be closed down and the copies of the magazines destroyed (*Sainath Prabha* Kiran 1, 1919).

The growing tension between D.B.S. and other devotees led to the paucity of funds, which affected the publication of the magazine and it was stopped for one year after May 1917.

From the side of the D.B.S., Keshavrao Deshpande, the chitnis, was present in Dwarkamayi when the matter was discussed with Sai Baba. Listening to the comments of Tatya, Sai Baba asked the view of the chitnis. Sai Baba heard the view of the chitnis and said that the Sanstha should continue.

Sainath Prabha resumed publication in May 1918. In this issue, Laxman Balwant Pethkar, B.A., L.L.B., High Court advocate, has been shown as the editor. He continued to be the editor till the publication magazine's last issue.[24]

Unfortunately, Sai Baba entered Mahasamadhi on 15th October 1918.[25] There was no one to guide the rival groups and diffuse the issues. Further, Sathe earlier had a physical bout in 1917 with a dreaded ascetic called Nanavali who threatened to kill him. Heeding to the advice of Kelkar, his father-in-law, he did not visit Shirdi as long as Nanavali was there. In his absence, D.B.S. virtually became non-functional for all practical purposes. Later, D.B.S. got amalgamated with Shri Sainath Sansthan Committee (S.S.S.C.) in October 1918.[26] This subsequently led to the formation of Shri Saibaba Sansthan Trust, Shirdi, in 1922.

Sainath Prabha: Special Facets

The November and December 1918 issues of Sainath Prabha were published shortly after Sai Baba's Mahasamadhi. An obituary was published in the November 1918 issue[27] and the cover page is captioned as "Shri Sainath Prabha" or "Dharma Rahasya" in Marathi. Below the words "Dharma Rahasya", the title *Shri Sainath Prabha* is mentioned. Shri Laxman Balvant Pethkar, an advocate of the High Court, continued to be the editor. It was priced at six annas per issue and ₹3 was the advance annual subscription. The names of the subscribers and the amount of subscription from each of them are mentioned in the initial pages of the magazine.[28]

Unlike the earlier issues which gave a lot of coverage to the activities pertaining to Sai Baba, the issues after his Mahasamadhi published only two articles about him out of the total eleven articles. The January 1919 issue carries two articles in English and nine in Marathi. From the research point of view, two articles are useful. They are 1) Sainath Dakshina Bhiksha Sanstha (pages 8–11) and 2) Shri Samarth Sainath Maharajanchya Aakhyayika (pages 16–17).

Since almost all the previous issues of this magazine were published when Sai Baba was in Shirdi in physical form, most of the news and themes mentioned can be taken to be based on first-hand information. Some information regarding Sai Baba's daily routine at Shirdi, divine personality and activities published in *Sainath Prabha* contain more details than any other book or publication. Hence, the merit of these magazines should not be underestimated simply because, as the organ of Dakshina Bhiksha Sanstha, it became controversial.

The important highlights of this magazine are given here. Since the writers of this magazine, including H.V. Sathe, had the privilege of communicating with Sai Baba and witnessing his activities, they could record and report the words of Sai Baba spoken in various contexts in rustic Marathi in the magazine. While some of these have been quoted by some writers in their books, many of them do not find a mention in any book, including *Shri Sai Satcharita*. Hence, the magazine is very important.

During the period of publication of *Sainath Prabha*, many important incidents and events happened around Sai Baba. While the details regarding some of these events are not mentioned in the available literature on Sai Baba, they have been reported in great detail in *Sainath Prabha*. Only cryptic references have been made in some books and articles about a few of the incidents. *Sainath Prabha* goes a long way in filling gaps in information and provides vital details.

Sainath Prabha was the first organized attempt to propagate the philosophy of Sai Baba through a magazine of this standard. The famous newspaper *Kesari*, founded by Lokmanya Bal Gangadhar Tilak, and *Sainath Prabha* were printed in the same press.

A few key details given here, gleaned from perusing the various issues of the magazine are of significance to all Sai devotees, researchers and readers:

- Details about the daily routine and lifestyle of Sai Baba in Shirdi including his movements.

- The celebration of Ramnavami in Shirdi – details of arrangements including those made by the D.B.S. and others like the police and other government agencies.

- Details about the Chawadi procession.

- The involvement of the District Administration of Ahmednagar, its Collector P.J. Mead, Assistant Collector and the chitnis to the Collector, K.R. Deshpande, in the affairs of Shirdi including that of D.B.S.

- Sai Baba is quoted as saying that Shirdi along with Nimgaon, Rahata, Rui, Pimpalgaon, Kopargaon and so on have been given to him by his Malik (Allah). Many mystic, unintelligible statements of Sai Baba also find a mention in the magazine.[29]

- Sai Baba's philosophy on dakshina – detailed information about dakshina doled out by him to his devotees including Tatya and Bade Baba[30] and many others.

- The attitude of some of those who benefited financially on the question of sharing even a portion of it for fulfilling Sai Baba's daily needs.

- The piquant situation faced by Sai Baba due to the demands of some greedy devotees and his attitude of saintly detachment amid the hustle-and-bustle of the worldly life around him.

- Genesis, growth and dissolution of D.B.S. including *Sainath Prabha*.

- A critical assessment on the role of sevakaris and mankaris in the Durbar Mandal of Sai Baba.

- Details about an attempt by D.B.S. to introduce a modern accounting system in order to manage the receipts and expenditures of Sai Baba, with the profit-and-loss book as appendage to the magazine, as an example.

- Description about certain unusual activities of Shankar Narayan Joshi/Vaidya alias Nanavali at Shirdi.

- The October and November 1918 issues deal with the information about Sai Baba's Mahasamadhi and thereafter.

- The death of Radhakrishna Ayi (in November 1916), under odd and suspicious circumstances and what followed her death.

- Information about the system of management of Sai Baba's estate and personal property after Mahasamadhi.

- Formation of S.S.S.C., later leading to the formation of Shri Saibaba Sansthan Trust.

- Publication of two interesting serial articles in Marathi titled "Shri Sainath Katha Karandaka" and "Laghu Yoga Vasishta".

Sainath Prabha: A Vital Source of Evidence about Shri Sai Baba and Shirdi

The publication of a bilingual magazine (in Marathi and English) in the year 1916, when Sai Baba was physically there at Shirdi, may be considered to be a unique feat especially given the context described so far. Those days, there would not have been many bilingual magazines of this standard published even from Mumbai or Pune.

A review of the various issues of this magazine, highlights the following social benefits that it had rendered:

- It was the only magazine that was published from Shirdi when Sai Baba was in his physical embodiment. The published issues contain some of the events at Shirdi between December 1915 and October 1919. Thus, it became a link between the pre-Samadhi and post-Samadhi period of Sai Baba. It provides some information about the changes that took place in Shirdi immediately after Sai Baba's Mahasamadhi.

- The Marathi speaking folks of the rural areas got a chance to read about Sai Baba. If we scan the list of subscribers, we find that it also includes a large number of urban readers from places like Mumbai, Nasik and Aurangabad. The elite class of these places came to know about the saintly character and the philanthropic activities of Sai Baba.

- Being published in English and Marathi, it could be read by Britishers and even English-speaking people living in Maharashtra and outside. This was the time when the British had introduced English as the official language in India. All those who mattered in the society or were holding high positions in the government, had to learn English. It is presumed that the officers of British origin and also the personnel of the police and detective departments, deployed to keep a watch in Shirdi due to the movement of persons like Khaparde, who was the close associate of Lokmanya Bal Gangadhar Tilak, must have kept a watch on the contents of this magazine as it contained vital information for their use.

- The magazine gave the devotees of Sai Baba staying at different places an opportunity to exchange their views and get connected. The magazine encouraged creation of Sai literature in the form of articles contributed for publication.

- Since the magazine was dedicated to the cause of Sai Baba, it was prepared with a lot of care by the devotees. Hence, the excellence in its quality is clearly discernible. Some common items of an ordinary magazine like advertisements and official court notices are not found in this magazine. It is extremely difficult to publish a magazine of this quality without earning some money from advertisements. This, perhaps, is one of the reasons why the magazine could not last long.

- The various issues of the magazine give a clear picture about life at Shirdi around Sai Baba. It feels like a live history of Sai Baba and of Shirdi between the years 1916 and 1919.

*****

Notes

1. *Shri Sai Leela* (Issue 1(i), 1930: back cover).

2. *Sant Kathamrut* and *Bhakta-Leelamrut* by Dasganu Maharaj; *Shri Sainath Bhajanmala* by Raguhnath and Savitri Tendulkar, *Bhakta Vijay* and *Sant Vijay* by Mahipati.

3. *Shri Sai Satcharita* by Govind Raghunath Dabholkar; *Devotees Experiences* by Narasimha Swami.

4. In 1878, Vishnushastri Krushnashastri Chiplunkar established a printing press by the name Aryabhushan Press at Poona, Maharashtra, India. Later, in the nineteenth century, Bal

Gangadhar Tilak's English newspaper *Kesari* was printed at this press followed by *Sainath Prabha*.

5. "In December 1915, I got a call from Baba, when I was at Poona and at his bidding, I helped in forming the above Society. I was made the President of it. We ran the journal *Sainath Prabha* as its organ. This was not read to Baba previously or submitted for his approval" (Swami 2006: 124).

6. "Hardly any copies are traceable. Parts 1 and 2 which alone are now available give some account of the state of affairs that prevailed at Shirdi Sansthan in 1915 to 1917 or 1918" (Swami 2006: 124).

7. *Sainath Prabha* Kiran 1, 1916: Publisher's Note.

8. Kher (2013: ix).

9. Gunaji (2002: 11).

10. Gunaji (2002: 9).

11. Swami (2006: 112).

12. *Sainath Prabha* (Kiran 2, 1916: 33).

13. Ganesh Shrikrishna Khaparde: *The Shirdi Diary of Ganesh Shrikrishna Khaparde*; Kakasaheb Dixit: *Kakasaheb Dixit Diary*.

14. "Such constituents of the vicious characters that, even Shree Sai Daya-Moorty's frequent reprimands now and then, seemed to be powerless to mend matters. The poor bhaktas, found perhaps in their helpless condition, no effective salvation; much less the confused villagers, who but gaped wildly with wondering eyes!" (*Sainath Prabha* Kiran 1, 1916: 15–16).

15. *Sainath Prabha* (Kiran 1, 1916: 33).

16. *Sainath Prabha* (Kiran 1, 1916: Cover page).

17. *Sainath Prabha* (Kiran 5, 1918: Cover page).

18. *Sainath Prabha* (Kiran 1, 1916).

19. "Necessary help from the Government to preserve order and peace, and the provision of all available facilities, for boarding, lodging, and darshan of Shree Sai Baba, from the Dakshina Bhiksha Sanstha, Saiabad, are made, in addition to possible sanitary convenience" (*Sainath Prabha* Kiran 1, 1916: 3(ii)).

20. An appeal to the devotees of Shri Sainath Maharaj.
    Sainath Prabha: Six to twelve volumes of the publication will be published in a year. Those who will book in advance will be given 25 per cent discount. Postal charges will be extra.
    The statement about Shri Sainath fund is detailed in the first volume in the article captioned "Shri Sainath and Shirdi". Those seeking life membership can contact the address below.

    The articles and monetary donations offered to Baba
    Till date parcels used to be received by post of railways and money used to come by money order. In future these should be sent to the address given below.

    Shri Sainath Maharaj ki Photo
    Baba's photographs of different sizes are available. The desirous persons can place orders as per address given below.

    Shri Sainath Bhajan Mala
    Smt. Savitri Bai Raghunath Tendulkar, price 0-8-0 anna. Dakshina Bhiksha Sanstha 1 anna. Postal charges extra. Those desirous, can place orders at the address given below.
    Address – Secretary (Chitnis) Dakshina Bhiksha Sanstha
             Sai Aabad/ Shirdi,
             Post – Rahata
             Taluka – Kopergaon
             Dist – Ahmednagar.
21. *Sainath Prabha* (Kiran 2, 1916: An Appeal).
22. *Sainath Prabha* (Kiran 5, 1918: 1).
23. *Sainath Prabha* (Kiran 2, 1916: 35).
24. *Sainath Prabha* (Kiran 2, 1916: Cover page).
25. *Sainath Prabha* (Kiran 4, 1917: 129).
26. *Sainath Prabha* (Kiran 11, 1918).
27. *Sainath Prabha* (Kiran 11, 1918: 17).
28. *Sainath Prabha* (Kiran 11, 1918: Back of cover page).
29. "Many of His bhaktas have heard Him, often saying, that, this village, with three others, have been given to Him, by His Malik. (The Almighty God)" (*Sainath Prabha* Kiran 1, 1916: 1–2).

30. "In addition to unquestioned and respectable proximity for
     many hours of the day, he enjoys the rare benefit of having his
     meals in His Company, in addition to the daily bakshees of
     several tens of rupees out of the arpanned dakshinas received"
     (*Sainath Prabha* Kiran 2, 1916: 64).

     "Fakir Baba . . . receiving an estimated average figure amounting
     to, at least, half a lac of rupees, since his arrival" (*Sainath Prabha*
     Kiran 2, 1916: 66).

9

Shri Sai Leela Maasik Pustak

(1923 Onwards)

This chapter narrates the origin, content and contribution of Shri Sai Leela magazine, which was first published in 1923.

After Sai Baba's Mahasamadhi, Shri Saibaba Sansthan Trust was formed in 1922[1] to take care of his Samadhi and other places of religious sanctity attached with Sai Baba and to maintain the articles used by him or used for conducting his puja and aarti. It was also responsible for looking after the visiting pilgrims and holding regular puja and special functions at Shirdi.

The Sansthan also took up the publication of *Shri Sai Leela* magazine. It is the official organ of the Sansthan and was first published in 1923 in Marathi language.

Today, it is the most widely-circulated magazine dedicated to Sai Baba and is multi-lingual (photograph 9.1).

Shri Sai Leela Magazine: Purpose and Contents

We will do a detailed study of the first issue of the *Shri Sai Leela* magazine and the succeeding issues to establish a clear picture about its creation, format and purpose. This will also familiarize the readers with some concepts and terminologies which will enable them to understand the contents of the magazine better.

Photograph 9.1: Cover page of *Shri Sai Leela*
Year 1, Issue 1, 1923 (Shaka 1845)

The first edition of *Shri Sai Leela* magazine was published as Varsha 1, Issue 1, Chaitra Shaka 1845 (year 1923).[2] The address of the office of the publication is shown as Shri Sai Leela, Kacheri, 5 Turner Road, Bandra, V. B. Railway. Ramchandra Atmaram Tarkhad is stated to be the publisher and Laxman Ganesh Mahajani is named as the editor on the cover page.

In the first year *Shri Sai Leela* magazine had thirteen issues. This was so because the monthly publication followed the Hindu astrological calendar. According to the Hindu almanac, the year 1923 contained an extra month (adhik maas) of Jyeshtha. Hence, two issues were released for the month of Jyeshtha, which made it thirteen issues in all for the year 1923.[3]

The first issue has thirty-two pages plus a cover page and a back page. The front inner cover page has an index (photograph 9.2). The index lists:

  i. Mangalacharan

 ii. The purpose of the magazine

iii. Maharajanche Anubhav (Experiences with the Maharaj)

 iv. Scheme for the management of the Shirdi Sansthan,

  v. Some anecdotes pertaining to the divine activities of Sai Baba (that have already been published)

 vi. *Shri Sai Satcharita* with its Upodghaat (Introduction)

This page contains an appeal from the editor to the readers, informing them that the first issue is being sent to them free of cost, as a sample, in the hope that they will subscribe to it. It states that for those willing to become subscribers, an advance annual subscription fee of ₹3 and 6 annas (inclusive of postal charges) will be charged for the next monthly issue and which would be sent through Value Payable Post. However, it also states that the persons not desiring to subscribe, may kindly advise by return post so that the next issue of the monthly magazine would not be despatched to them.

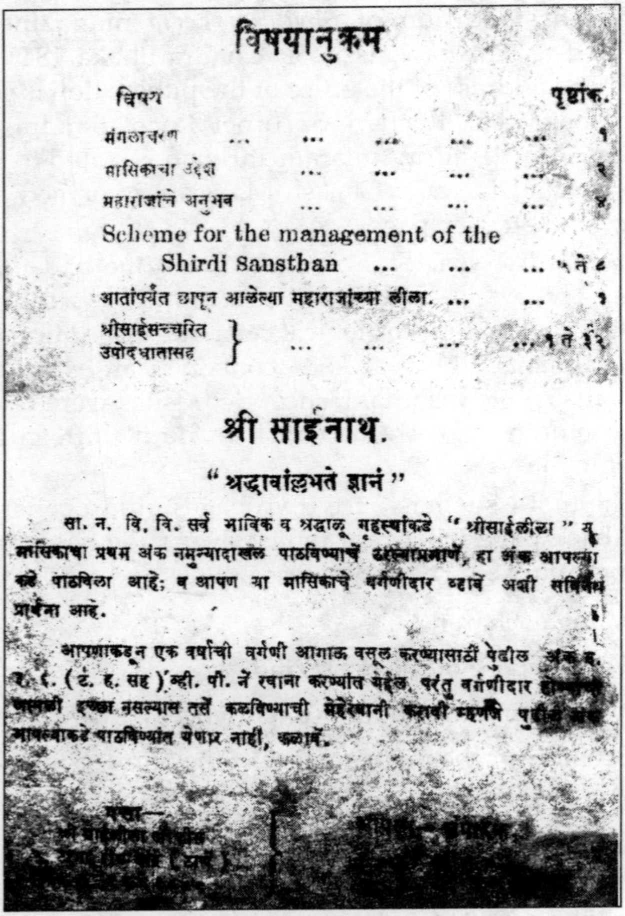

विषयानुक्रम

विषय	पृष्ठांक.
मंगलाचरण	१
मासिकाचा उद्देश	२
महाराजांचे अनुभव	४
Scheme for the management of the Shirdi Sansthan	५ ते ८
आतांपर्यंत छापून आलेल्या महाराजांच्या लीला.	१
श्रीसाईसच्चरित उपोद्धातासह	१ ते १२

श्री साईनाथ.

"श्रद्धावांल्लभते ज्ञानं"

सा. न. वि. वि. सर्व भाविक व श्रद्धाळू गृहस्थांकडे "श्रीसाईलीला" या मासिकाचा प्रथम अंक नमुन्यादाखल पाठविण्याचें ठरल्याप्रमाणें, हा अंक आपल्याकडे पाठविला आहे; व आपण या मासिकाचे वर्गणीदार व्हावें अशी सविनय प्रार्थना आहे.

आपणाकडून एक वर्षाची वर्गणी आगाऊ वसूल करण्यासाठीं पुढील अंक रु. २. ६. (ट. ह. सह) व्ही. पी. नें रवाना करण्यांत येईल. परंतु वर्गणीदार होण्याची आपली इच्छा नसल्यास तसें कळविण्याची मेहेरबानी करावी म्हणजे पुढील अंक आपल्याकडे पाठविण्यांत येणार नाहीं, कळावें.

Photograph 9.2: Back of cover page of *Shri Sai Leela*, 1923

The Manglacharan begins with:

> *"Sai Raham nazar karna, baccho ka palan karna"*
>
> and
>
> *"Raham azar karo ab more Sai"*[4]

The purpose of the magazine has been spelt out after that. The name of the magazine itself indicates its purpose. The magazine says that there are innumerable Sai Baba devotees spread all over. Sai Baba gives various experiences at different times to his devotees. These are still being experienced even after his Mahasamadhi. Devotees who have not seen Sai Baba in his human embodiment are also reported to be experiencing him. A shloka from Sai Baba's ashtak which is included in the daily aarti of Sai Baba (photograph 9.3) mentions about the inexplicable divine activities of Sai Baba.

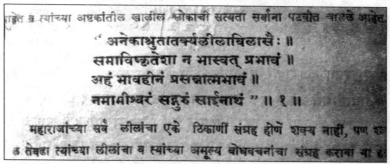

Photograph 9.3: Shri Sai Baba's ashtak mentioned under the caption "Masikacha Uddesh"

The meaning of the shloka is that many unheard-of divine sports, some of which are beyond reason, have manifested his shining divine glory. I bow to Sadguru Sainath who is devoid of ego and is full of the quality of inner happiness that is, happiness of the inner soul.

The article holds that it is impossible to compile all the experiences and leelas of Sai Baba. However, the main purpose of the magazine is to collect Sai Baba's leelas and bodh vachans and publish them. Every single word and leela of Sai Baba is for the upliftment and salvation of bhaktas and every single act has a meaning. It further states that the collection of his leelas is for the benefit of people at large and not restricted to his devotees alone. An effort is made to compile all the experiences and caption them as "Maharajenche Anubhav" and "Shri Sai Satcharita".

After obtaining permission from Sai Baba, a compilation of *Shri Sai Satcharita* was written in ovi (a Marathi word which means a stanza of a particular measure) form. Personal experiences sent by the devotees to the editor were published under "Maharajanche Anubhav".

In the first issue, the editor states that:

> A large number of such experiences are yet to be published. The readers are requested to point out mistakes, if any. As and when experiences of devotees are received, they will be suitably incorporated in the subsequent issues. Experience or upadesh imparted discreetly to a devotee will not be published. However, experiences given in public would be for the benefit of the public. It should be clearly understood by the Sai devotees that this is for the benefit of all and belongs to all.

Self-translated

The editor made a list of approximately 900 devotees. He requested other devotees, spread all over the country, to send their information so that it could be added to the list. He stated that the purpose of the service is for the continued remembrance of Sai Mauli.[5]

Under the heading "Maharajanche Anubhav", the first experience published was of Krishnaji Kashinath Joshi alias Bhau Maharaj.

Of all the articles contained in this issue, the article on the "Scheme for the Management of the Shirdi Sansthan of Shri Sai Baba" is most important from the point of view of writers and researchers. The resolution which conceptualised the scheme states that:

> All the Sansthan property both moveable and immovable shall vest in the following five trustees for life – Mr. Moreshwer Vishvanath Pradhan, B.A., L.L.B., Member Bombay Legislative Council; Mr. Lakshman Ganesh Mahajani of Messrs. Shoorji Vallabhdas & Co., Merchants Bombay; Prof. Ganesh Govind Narke, Professor of Chemistry and Geology, College of

Science, Poona; Ramchandra Atmaram Turkhud, Manager and Secretary, Khatau Makanji Mills, Bombay; and Mr. Tatya Ganpati Patil Kote, Land-holder, of Shirdi. Any vacancy in the trustees shall be filled by the rest of them as early as possible from among the Bhaktas of Shri Sai Baba subject to confirmation by the District Judge.

Shri Sai Leela Issue 1, 1923: 5 (Annexure-3)

We shall not elaborately deal with the history of the Shri Saibaba Sansthan Trust, Shirdi, in this book. Our main purpose is to deliberate on the *Shri Sai Leela* magazine.

In pages 1–21, there is an introduction to *Shri Sai Satcharita*, written by "babanche ek lekru" (a child of Baba), Hari Sitaram Dixit, under the title "Upodghaat". According to Dixit, "Baba came to Shirdi approx. 50 years ago", that is, fifty years before 1923, which is around 1873.[6] This is an important information regarding the arrival of Sai Baba in Shirdi.

This is followed by the chapter 1 of *Shri Sai Satcharita*. On the back page of the first issue, there is a notice advising the location from where *Shri Sadguru Sainath Sagunopasna* and *Shri Sainath Bhajanmala* could be procured.

The magazine further informs that Sai Baba's leelas have already been published by Smt. Savitri Bai Tendulkar as mentioned in the preface to her book *Shri Sainath Bhajanmala*. Some of the poems were written by Savitri Bai and some by her husband, Shri Raghunathrao Tendulkar. The leela mentioned in the preface pertains to the lighting of the lamps with water in Dwarkamayi Masjid.

It is worthwhile to know how and when the concept of *Shri Sai Leela* originated and who all were involved in this important venture. The publication of *Shri Sai Leela* magazine came at an opportune time. After the Mahasamadhi of Sai Baba, the devotees were frantically trying to recall the memories of Sai Baba. *Shri Sai Leela* magazine came like a divine grace and filled the vacuum.

The origin and the concept of *Shri Sai Leela* can be found in one of the subsequent articles written by Tarkhad, published in Year 8, Issue 13, Shaka 1853 (AD 1931), the gist of which is the following:

On one Sunday morning, almost nine years ago, Dabholkar came to his house with a handwritten manuscript of the chapters of *Shri Sai Satcharita*. Going through the initial chapters, Tarkhad found them to be very engrossing and captivating and requested Dabholkar to get all the chapters published.

Publishing the book involved expense and Dabholkar was anxious if the publication of such a book would be liked or not by people. Hence, following the advice of Hari Sitaram Dixit, it was decided that, to begin with, a monthly magazine would be published. Nothing happened for the next six months till one day Dabholkar and Dixit visited Tarkhad's house to discuss the plan for Samarth's Kayam fund. They decided to put together their own experiences and that of the other devotees, which would benefit other devotees. These would be published in the form of a monthly magazine using a fixed fund. A sum of ₹500 was drawn from Shri's fund and was handed over to Tarkhad to commence the publication of the monthly *Shri Sai Leela* magazine. The first issue of this monthly had 950 subscribers and due to its popularity another 1,000 copies had to be printed. A discussion between Dabholkar, Dixit and Tarkhad led to the conclusion that the publication of the book would not be cost effective. However, it was decided to publish a magazine within viable economic parameters, given the need of the devotees at that time.

Thus, it can be concluded that the original manuscript written by Dabholkar was initially published in the form of articles in various issues of *Shri Sai Leela* under the title *Shri Sai Satcharita*. It was later compiled and published in the form of the book *Shri Sai Satcharita* in the year 1930.[7]

Shri Sai Leela Magazine: Surmounting Challenges to Enable Continuity

Dixit used to search for the experiences of devotees, compile them and get them printed as long as he was alive. After his demise, many issues of *Shri Sai Leela* were delayed in printing. At the time of Dabholkar's death, the issue ran late by one year and the number of subscribers decreased from 950 to 400. After Dabholkar, the responsibility came on the shoulders of Tarkhad, a person who did not strive for fame or limelight. Bearing the burden of running *Shri Sai Leela* magazine, Tarkhad felt distressed. So M.W. Pradhan and B.V. Deo came to help him. Since he was not financially sound, Tarkhad made an appeal to the Sai devotees to contribute. Tarkhad made the following appeal to all Sai devotees:

> Today, at the age of seventy, still I have to work to meet my family expenses, and also bear other responsibilities. Moreover, Shirdi Saibaba Sansthan has entrusted upon me the work of a treasurer. I have a firm belief that everything is going on smoothly only because of Shri's grace . . . this meek person dedicates entire work of maintaining the subscribers of *Shri Sai Leela* at the feet of Sai Mauli. The only reason behind writing this detail is that the subscribers of *Shri Sai Leela* have now reduced to 250. After deducting the postal and printing expenses, I have to bear 200–250 from my own pocket instead of contributing anything to the fixed fund. Keeping all these things in mind all Sai devotees should consider that *Sai Leela* is for them and therefore should subscribe the magazine and be fortunate to contribute to Shri's fixed fund and oblige the Sansthan.

Shri Sai Leela Issue 13, 1931: 30–32, self-translated

Tarkhad wrote the following preface in the book of M.W. Pradhan:

> I feel pleasure in placing before the public this short sketch of the life and teachings of the late Divine Master, Shri Sai

Baba of Shirdi by Rao Bahadur Moreshwar Vishwanath
Pradhan of Sai Pradhan Baug, Santacruz. He has taken his
standpoint, by the translations of the various incidents in
Shri Sai Baba's life, as they have appeared in *Shri Sai Leela*,
a Marathi monthly journal written by the able pen of the
late Hon'ble Mr. Hari Sitaram Dixit, an eminent solicitor
of Mumbai, and an equally eminent and sturdy devotee of
Shri Sai Baba.

Pradhan 1943: 14

Shri Sai Leela magazine became a great success and
contributed a lot towards spreading Sai Baba's name far-
and-wide even though its publication went through rough
patches and lean periods due to various reasons.

A monthly journal, *Sai Lila* was started and Baba was pleased
to keep up some degree of Sai bhakti amongst those who
had contacted him and the small number that came
into contact through them. As decades after decade
went on, this way of keeping up Sai bhakti appeared
to fail, and that is why Abdulla Jan noted in 1936 that
the number of persons approaching Sai Baba at Shirdi
was so pitiably small on ordinary occasions.

Swami 1994a: 261

Shri Sai Leela Magazine: Providing the Basis for the Massive Growth in Sai Literature

After some years of publication, some devotees, particularly
from South India, requested an English section in the
magazine. Subsequently, people asked for an English
edition as well.[8]

In the meantime, a lot of changes and improvements
were taking place in the publication of the magazine.
According to the information given in www.sai.org.in, it
became a monthly magazine, published in Marathi, Hindi
and English.

Further, the magazine has been archived from the year 1923 to 2018. Details of enrolment and subscription for the magazine can be found at www.sai.org.in.

Subscription rates of the printed version as mentioned on the official website are shown in table 9.1.

Table 9.1: Subscription rates of the printed version of Shri Sai Leela as last updated on the official website of Shri Saibaba Sansthan Trust, Shirdi

Particulars	Amount (in Indian Rupees)
Annual (India)	50/-
Life Membership (India)	1,000/-
Annual (Foreign Edition including Postage)	1,000/-
Single Copy (India)	8/-

Shri Sai Leela magazine is the first official journal of Shri Saibaba Sansthan Trust, Shirdi, which started publishing documents on Sai Baba's life history and philosophy. From the year 1923 till now, this magazine has been an effective instrument in carrying forward the Sai heritage and culture.

Today the number of magazines about Sai Baba, in India and abroad, printed and online, are too numerous to be listed. We can find such magazines and journals in almost all the Indian languages. Credit to starting this goes to *Sainath Prabha* and *Shri Sai Leela*. As already discussed, *Sainath Prabha* (published from 1916 to 1919) was the first magazine exclusively dedicated to Sai Baba. The second magazine covering the same subject was *Shri Sai Leela*, published by Shri Saibaba Sansthan Trust, Shirdi in 1923. *Sainath Prabha* was bilingual and *Shri Sai Leela* was initially only in Marathi. Later, *Shri Sai Leela* was published in Hindi and English versions as well.

*****

Notes

1. "The permission for the scheme of management was approved by the Ahmednagar district court on 13-02-1922. Subsequently the district court officer Shri Parkhe visited Shirdi and handed over all the articles and belongings etc. of Sansthan to Tatya Ganpat Rao Patil Kote and other trustees" (*Shri Sai Leela* Issue 8, 1923: 50, self-translated).
2. "In collaboration with Govind Dabholkar, Hari Dixit launched a Marathi journal called *Shri Sai Leela* in 1923. The sketch originally appeared in the first volume of this journal. The journal project was an outcome of the Sai Baba Sansthan, created by Dixit at Shirdi after the saint's death" (Shepherd 2017: 71).
3. As per Hindu calendar Shaka 1845 (AD 1923) had 13 months.
4. "*Sai raham nazar karna, baccho ka palan karna*" meaning: Sai, please cast your kind glances and rear your children. "*Raham nazar karo ab more Sai*" meaning: My Sai, please cast your kind glances. These prayers, composed by Dasganu, form a part of the Kakad Aarti (morning aarti) conducted daily in all Sai Baba temples.
5. *Shri Sai Leela* (Issue 1, 1923: 2–3).
6. Ibid: 1.
7. *Shri Sai Leela* (Issue 13, 1931: 30–31).
8. "In the English section of *Sai Leela* magazine, some articles about Sai Baba appeared in 1943. Some South Indian devotees wrote to the then editor, Mr. S.N. Kharkar, suggesting that *Shri Sai Satcharita*, being in Marathi, was a sealed book to them and that it would be better if the purport of the chapters of that book be published in seriatim in the English section of *Sai Leela*. The editor requested Shri N.V. Gunaji to undertake this work and by Sai Baba's grace, he did it as part of his service to Him. By Baba's inspiration and guidance, the work was completed by the end of 1944, but owing to the scarcity of paper, as well as the Paper Control Regulations under the Defence of India Rules, the publication was delayed for some time" (Keller: 24).

Annexures

Annexure-1

Kakasaheb Dixit's letter to the Collector and District Magistrate, Ahmednagar dated 22nd October 1918 about the death of Sai Baba of Shirdi and requesting that his property be handed over to the Committee which had been formed to conduct the worship of the Sai Baba's tomb

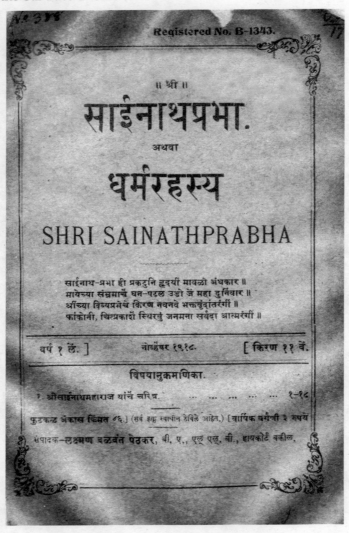

Registered No. B-1343.

॥ श्री ॥

साईनाथप्रभा.

अथवा

धर्मरहस्य

SHRI SAINATHPRABHA

साईनाथ-प्रभा ही प्रकटुनि ह्रदयीं मावळो अंधकार ॥
मायेच्या संभ्रमाचें घन-पटल उडो जें महा दुर्निवार ॥
श्रींच्या विश्वप्रसेंचें किरण नवनवे भक्तचूंदांतरंगीं ॥
फांकोनी, चित्रप्रकाशीं स्थिरतु जनमना खवेदा आत्मरंगीं ॥

वर्ष १ लें.]   नोव्हेंबर १९१८.   [किरण ११ वें.

विषयानुक्रमणिका.

१ श्रीसाईनाथमहाराज यांचें चरित्र. १-१८

कुटकन अंकाच किंमत ८६.] (सर्व हक्क स्वाधीन ठेविले आहेत.) [वार्षिक वर्गणी ३ रुपये

संपादक—लक्ष्मण बळवंत पेठकर, बी. ए., एल् एल्. बी., हायकोर्ट वकील.

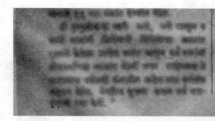

(मे॰ कलेक्टरसाहेबांकडे केलेला अर्ज)
Shirdi.

To,

THE COLLECTOR AND DISTRICT
MAGISTRATE,
AHMEDNAGAR.

Sir,

On behalf of and as directed by the
Shri Sainath Sansthan Committee I beg

साईनाथमहाराज यांच चरित्र

to inform you with deep regret that His
Holiness Shri Sai Baba of Shirdi breathed His last on Tuesday the 15th instant. His remains were put unt to His
wishes buried in the stately wada
which Shrimant Gopalrao Mukund Buti
commenced building under the orders of
His Holiness and which is st ll under
constru tion. His Holiness had a very
large number of devotees and His shrine
will be worshipped by people of all
classes. As the shrine will be a permanent institution it was teemed necessary
to have a body to manage the same and
the under-mentioned persons were according y constituted into a Committee
f r the purpose of managing the said
institution, under the name of Shri Sainath Sansthan Committee and the Dakshina Bhiksha Sar stha has been amalgamated with it. The names and descript
tions of the persons consti uting the sai-
committee are as under :—

1. Shrimant G. M. Buti, a very rich
Banker of Nagpur who has settled
down at Shirdi and proprietor of
the Wada where the said shrine is
located, President of the Committee
now constituted as aforesaid.
2. Mr. Narayan Govind Chandorkar
retired Deputy Collector.
3. Rao Bahadur Hari Vinayak Sathe
retired Superintendent of Land Records and President of the Dakshina
Bhiksha Committee which had the
custody of the bulk of His Holiness'
property during His lif -time.
4. Mr. Hari Sitaram Dixit, Solicitor
and at one time an additional member of the Bombay Legislative
Council.
5. Mr. Moreshwar Wishwanath Pradhan B A. LL. B. Pleader. High
Court. a well-known devotee of His
Holiness
6. Mr. Sakharam Hari Jog retired
Sub-Engineer.
7. Mr. Purushottam Sakharam Bhate
retired mamlatdar.
8. Mr. Shankarao Raghunath Desh-

pande who was for several years
Honorary Mag'strate Sangamner.
9. Mr. Laks man Balwant Peebkar B.A.
LL. B. High Court Pleader, who
is a devo'ee of His Holiness and
who has under His Holiness' orders
been the Editor and General Mana
ger of the Monthly religious Magazine called the Sainath Prabha or
Dharma Rahasya.
10. Mr. Ganesh Damodar Kelkar a
great devotee of His Holiness who
has settled down in Shirdi and who
is the Secretary of the said Daxina
Bhiksha Committee.
11. Dr. Chidambaram Pillay retired
Veterinary Inspector Central Provinces and a member of the Shirdi
Sanitary Committee.
12. Mr. Tatya bin Ganpati Patil Kote
Chairman Shirdi Sanitary Committee.
13. Ramchandra bin Dada Kote member Shirdi Sanitary Committee.
14. Mr. Mahadeorao Balvant Deshpande member Shirdi Sanitary
Committee.
15. Fatia Baba Pai Mohomed a leading member of the Mohomedan
Comnnty and payer of income tax
at Shirdi.

I am directed further to i nform you
that the property left by His Holiness
consists of articles diedicated to his
Holiness from time to time by his devotees as a'sy of articles purchased by Him
for His own use. The said property
may be divi ted un ler the following heads.

(a) Articles used for the worship
of His Holiness.

(b) Articles of precessional paraphernalia inc'uding Horse,
palanquin, Rath etc.

(c) Articles personally used by His
Holiness and which will be
preserved as sacred relics and
worshipped by His Holiness'
devotees.

साईनाथप्रभा

(d) Sundries such as cooking pots water pots, clock etc.

All the property left by His Holiness has at present been taken charge of by the Mamlatdar of Kopargaon for safe custody. Now however that a Committee for managing the said shrine has been constituted, I am directed by the said committee to request you to be so good as to order that the entire property of His Holiness be delivered to President of the Shri Sainath Sansthan Committee.

I beg to remain.

Sir,

Your most obedient servant

(Sd) HARI SITARAM DIXIT.

Endorsement by Rao Bahadur Hari Vinayak Sathe. " The above has my full concurrence and as President of the Daxina Bhiksha Sanstha, I would earnestly pray that the entire property of His Holiness may be handed over to Mr. Butti as requested above. "

(Sd) HARI VINAYAK SATHE.

मे. कलेक्टर साहेब यांचे उत्तर

Application of Mr. Hari Sitaram Dixit endorsed by Rao Bahadur H. V. Sathe dated 2? October informing the Collector of the death of Shri Sai Baba of Shirdi and requesting that his property be handled to a committee which has been formed to conduct the worship of the deceased's tomb.

Read Mamlatdar of Kopargaon's report on the subject

ORDER

The deceased was a Mahomedan of unknown origin who came to Shirdi and gained a reputation of great sanctity, being worshipped by Hindus as well as Mahomedans. He died intestate and a committee has formed itself to continue the worship of the deceased as a saint. It consists of a number of Hindu gentlemen of high position and one Mahomedan. After some dispute the deceased was buried with Mahomedan rites in a Wada built for the purpose by a Hindu gentleman.

The Mamlatdar has taken charge of the property under section 57 of the District Police Act. There is no provision for me to hand over the property to any committee. In view of the possibility of dissensions it is most advisable to have the matter legally settled. The only legal course is for me to report under section 58 of the District Police Act to the District Judge. It is open to the committee to make immediately to the District Judge any application they wish for the temporary disposal of the property pending his final orders. In order to cause no delay a copy of this order is to be sent to Mr. Hari Sitaram Dikshit as well as to the District Judge.

(Sd) C. A. BEYTS,

District Magistrate, Ahmednagar.

No. D. M. 158 of 1918.

Ahmednagar, 24th October 1918.

Copy forwarded to

Mr. HARI SITARAM DIKSHIT.

(Sd) C. A. BEYTS.

District Magistrate, Ahmednagar.

येणें प्रमाणें हकीगत झाली. पुढें होणारी हकीगत कमाकमानें पुढील अंकीं प्रसिद्ध करण्यांत येईल. असो. पुढील अंकापासून वाचकांचे धार्मिक विषय पूर्ववत येतील, इतकें सांगून वाचकांची रजा घेऊन हा सर्व लेख समयें वाचकांचे चरणीं समर्पण करितों.

Printed at the Aryabhushan Press by Anant Vinayak Patvardhan, at Poona City and Published by
Laxman Balvant Petkar, B. A. LL. B., High Court Vakil for the Shri Sainath Dakshina Bhiksha Sanstha, Sristhal of Shirdi. Tal. Kopargaon, Dist. Ahmednagar, at 29 A Kasba Peth, Poona City.

Annexure-2

Cleveland Report 1909, Government of India, Political-Deposit Proceedings, June 1909 no. 3

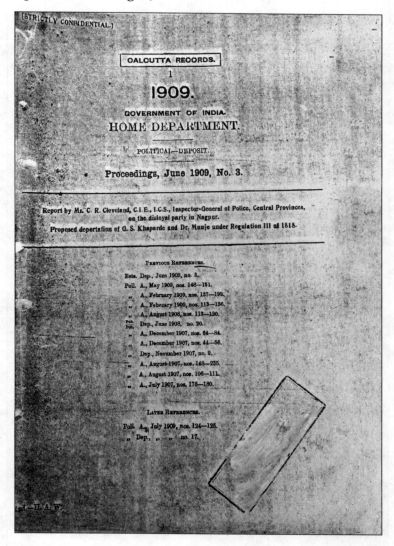

[STRICTLY CONFIDENTIAL.]

CALCUTTA RECORDS.

1

1909.

GOVERNMENT OF INDIA.

HOME DEPARTMENT.

POLITICAL—DEPOSIT.

Proceedings, June 1909, No. 3.

Report by Mr. C. R. Cleveland, C.I.E., I.C.S., Inspector-General of Police, Central Provinces, on the disloyal party in Nagpur.

Proposed deportation of G. S. Khaparde and Dr. Munje under Regulation III of 1818.

PREVIOUS REFERENCES.

Esta. Dep., June 1909, no. 3.

Poll. A., May 1909, nos. 146—151.

    „ A., February 1909, nos. 137—199.

    „ A., February 1909, nos. 113—136.

    „ A., August 1908, nos. 115—130.

    Poll. Dep., June 1908, no. 20.

    „ A., December 1907, nos. 64—84.

    „ A., December 1907, nos. 44—56.

    „ Dep., November 1907, no. 9.

    „ A., August 1907, nos. 148—235.

    „ A., August 1907, nos. 106—111.

    „ A., July 1907, nos. 178—180.

LATER REFERENCES.

Poll. A., July 1909, nos. 124—125.

    „ Dep., „ „ no. 17.

1—H.A.W.

NOTES.

POLITICAL—D:, JUNE 1909.

No. 3.

REPORT BY Mr. C. R: CLEVELAND; C.I.E:, I.C.S., INSPECTOR-GENERAL OF POLICE CENTRAL PROVINCES ON THE DISLOYAL PARTY IN NAGPUR. PROPOSED DEPORTATION OF G. S. KHAPARDE AND Dr. MUNJE, UNDER REGULATION III OF 1818..

Demi-official from the Honourable Mr. R. H. Craddock, to Sir Harold Stuart, dated the 19th March 1909.

I am sending a report* by Cleveland on the disloyal party in Nagpur. He is just about to make some enquiries into their organization in Berar. A note of my own on the situation accompanies, and I should like you to put the Report and Note before the Government of India for their consideration.

*Vide unprinted papers.

2. The statements made by the principal disloyalists to Cleveland were (with the great reservation regarding their real plans of exciting to violence) astonishingly frank. Upon the news of the deportations in Bengal they became extraordinarily milder and made little or no fuss about the stopping of the Congress. Their papers temporarily collapsed, and, as Mr. Chitnavis said, " There had not been such peace in Nagpur for a long time." But they have begun, as I anticipated, to pluck up courage, and I am therefore taking proceedings under section 108 against the *Deshasewak* for defaming Judges, and under section 124-A against a new paper in Akola, the *Swalamban*. These prosecutions, however, are not of any permanent use, because they only touch foolish tools for whom it is impossible not to feel some sympathy, while all the prime movers and conspirators remain concealed behind.

3. Whether that arch rebel Khaparde will venture to come back or not, I do not know It is in my opinion most essential that he should never set his foot in Berar again. His return would be a signal for a general recrudescence of violent oratory, schoolboy indiscipline, and general disloyalist activities. The disloyal people are now on the tack of Mahar schools, and night schools for *hamals*. Their idea is to get at the undisciplined masses; as they did with the mill hands of Bombay. Education and religion will be their two cloaks in future. Leaders and funds are their two requirements, and it is leaders like Khaparde who are the chief means of securing the funds. Khaparde's deportation will therefore be a tremendous blow. As regards the lieutenants and petty officers of Khaparde's army, I should like to be able to call them up and tell them that if they do not cease from troubling, we shall deport one or two of them after they have had a fair interval for repentance, and one or two more from time to time if they continue to misbehave.

The owner of the seditious press must risk his capital; the seditious pleader his license ; and the seditious leader his liberty. If we do not do this we must slowly but surely abrogate our authority. Our reforms are not at present wanted by the 99 per cent. that make up the masses ; but they are required to keep the *literati* of the classes contented. Of the one per cent. English *literati* at least four-fifths will be satisfied by them, and do not want anything more, or worry about Colonial systems. The remaining fifth may constitute the disloyal party. Therefore, for the sake of five people in a thousand (but I am not sure that it is really more than one in five thousand) are we to hold our hands and let them work their wicked will, poisoning the masses, corrupting the youth, ostensibly in the sacred name of liberty, but really in the hope of self-aggrandizement and power to oppress? Are we to do this well knowing their inefficiency, their dishonesty, and their hostility to our Government and desire to overthrow it ?

4. The National Congress must either drop its Colonial *Swaraj* creed, or cease to exist. How long are we going to listen to this nonsense about *Swaraj* on the colonial system, which, as I have tried to show in my Note, is an impossible ideal ! These men only do these things as long as they think there is reasonable safety. Even deportation loses its terrors if the deportee comes back again in a short time. I would give the intended deportee fair warning, give him time to amend his ways, watch him and leave him a *locus penitentiae* But there must be a sword of Democles over him and when it falls, the blow must strike home

131 H.T

11

6. The Bombay High Court have given a most useful lead in adding a note to pleaders'
Poll. Dep., July 1909, no. 17. licenses to the effect that participation in a
disloyal movement may lead to revocation of his
license. Mr. Craddock will no doubt move the Judicial Commissioner to take similar action.

7. I need not touch on the educational question, the solution of which requires a large expenditure of money which we have not got at present.

8. We may agree that the Chief Commissioner had sound grounds for prohibiting the Congress assembly at Nagpur. I think that the case should be circulated for information.

H. A[DAMSON],—7-4-09.

The papers are very interesting and should be circulated. It would be altogether inopportune to raise the question of deportation under present conditions.

M[INTO],—23-4-09.

I have seen these papers with much interest.

2. I agree generally in Mr. Craddock's reading of the facts. The disloyalists, as he calls them, have undoubtedly for some years past been active in the Central Provinces in laying the foundation of widespread hatred to the Government and its agents, with results of which the seriousness will be recognized when the next periodical wave of general discontent passes over the country.

3. Comparatively small, however, as the number of persons actively engaged in this propaganda may be, I do not believe that we can permanently put it down by continuous resort to repressive measures, such as the Chief Commissioner recommends, even if such a system were open to us, which it is not. We can produce a great effect temporarily by special measures, such as deportations. That has been shown clearly enough in the Punjab and Eastern Bengal, but in neither case is there that evidence of permanent improvement in the state of feeling that one would like to see. The Lieutenant Governor of Eastern Bengal has in several of his recent reports warned us not to believe too much in the superficial signs of improvement, and the tone of the Vernacular Press in the Punjab, though more restrained in expression than before, shows very little less real bitterness.

4. I agree that special measures must be kept for special occasions and that there is nothing in the general position in the Central Provinces that would justify the deportation of Khaparde and Munje. At the same time I think we could probably make out quite as strong a case against the former at least of these two, as against some of the others whom we have deported; and if conditions should change and we should in the Central Provinces have to face the same overt acts of hostility that we have had in Bengal, there is probably no measure that would have a more immediate effect than the arrest of Khaparde, if he should return. Our reply to the Chief Commissioner should, I think, be sufficiently non-committal to leave us a free hand in Khaparde's case, if action should ever be necessary. It will be very satisfactory if he stays in England.

5. I entirely agree in all that has been said about improving the position of Educational Department especially in secondary schools. This is, I think, an urgently wanted reform.

J. O. M[ILLER].—26-4-09.

I agree on the merits of the case with the Honourable Mr. Miller.

2. I think the Secretary of State's private telegram of 30th November 1908 should be
Poll. A., Feb, 1909, nos. 137-199. made official, and that local Governments should be
acquainted, if they are not so already, of the
restrictions which have been placed in the working of the regulation. This would enable them, in times of emergency, to have the cases sent up complete.

W. L. H[ARVEY],—26-4-09.

Deportation seems to me to be, at any rate at present, quite out of the question.

I agree in the main with Sir Harold Stuart's admirable note.

G. F. W[ILSON],—26-4-09.

I have read a good portion of Mr. Cleveland's report* and the whole of the letter of the
*Vide unprinted papers. Chief Commissioner of the Central Provinces and I
have come to the conclusion that there is not, at present, a case for deportation against either Dr. Munje or Mr. Khaparde, should the latter come back to India.

I agree generally in the conclusions of the Honourable Sir Harvey Adamson and Sir Harold Stuart.

S. P. S[INHA],—27-4-09.

7

source. Preventive action is just as much required for securing the peace of the country as punitive measures which from their nature must often be fitful and sometimes unsuccessful, while they generally fail entirely in reaching the prime movers.

17. The educated loyalist requires some sort of legitimate and constitutional means and place in which he can raise his voice and proclaim his opinion, and in all the large Provinces the new reforms will supply the time and the place for gratifying these legitimate aspirations. It is for this reason that I have also recommended an Advisory Council for the Central Provinces and Berar. But with these means supplied there is no room left consistently with the maintenance of the British Government for a National Congress and a National creed, and those professing loyalists who still desire to lead or support such a Congress must be told this in unmistakable terms. Presidency or Provincial Associations there may reasonably be for making representations on particular bills, particular taxes, or particular measures ; but any congress, body, or association which sets before itself some scheme of government, which is not the constitutional government of India as by law established, must be made to disappear. As long as we give any sort of recognition to the National Congress with a creed of colonial or any other *Swaraj*, we are tolerating, and letting the people see that we are tolerating, an organization which has as its chief object the overthrow of the British Raj.

18. The Chief Commissioner of the Central Provinces and Berar governs a Province only eighth in importance in British India, and it may seem to the Government of India that I have gone beyond my own sphere in raising the questions which are raised in this note ; but I have very firm convictions on this subject, and as the photographs obtained by Mr. Cleveland show there is a combination between Calcutta, Barisal, Poona, Delhi and Nagpur, and I consider that I should do wrong if I did not state my convictions plainly to the Government of India. I have only served in one Province, but I have watched these movements in close touch both with the educated and the masses for twenty years, and I can bear personal testimony to the astonishing rapidity with which the enemy of the British Government has advanced from point to point during the last five years. We may have only to compare Khaparde's speech in 1905 (page 28 of

* *Vide* unprinted papers.

Mr. Cleveland's report)* with his and B. C. Pal's *Swaraj* manifesto (appendix J of the annexures) to appreciate what a change has come over the spirit of the agitator. That which was whispered with bated breath in the inmost chambers of Poona has now been proclaimed far and wide over the land and is on the lips of every school-boy when he shouts the cry of "Bande Mataram."

R. H. CRADDOCK,

Chief Commissioner, Central Provinces.

I have glanced through the papers. Send on to Sir H. Stuart. I fear that there is no case strong enough for deportation in the Central Provinces at present.

H. A[DAMSON],—27-3-09.

Submitted for orders with reference to the proposal made in paragraphs 10 and 11 of the Chief Commissioner's note to deport Khaparde and Dr. Munje. We have no papers about Mr. Ker tells me the Director, Criminal these two persons, but Director of Criminal Intelli-Intelligence's papers are in Simla. gence has probably got files about them.

H. G. STOKES.

2. In considering the Chief Commissioner's proposal attention is invited to the following papers :—

Pub.—Poll. A., Dec. 1907, nos. 44-56.

(1) Paragraph 1 of Secretary's note, dated 21st June 1907.

(2) Secretary of State's telegram, dated 1st July 1907.

Pub.—Poll. A., Aug. 1907, nos. 148-235.

(3) Sir Erle Richards' note dated 5th May 1907.

(4) Paragraph 4 of Secretary's note dated 11th July 1907.

Pub.—Poll. A., Aug. 1907, nos. 100-111.

(5) His Excellency's note, dated 13th July 1907.

(6) The portion marked in His Excellency's note, dated 27th July 1908.

Poll. A., Aug. 1908, nos. 113-120.

(7) Paragraph 7 of Sir Erle Richards' note dated 3rd August 1908.

Poll. A., Feb. 1909, nos. 187-199.

(8) Secretary of State's private telegram, dated 30th November 1908.

Annexure-3

Scheme for the management of the Shirdi Sansthan of Shri Sai Baba as in *Shri Sai Leela* 1923

SCHEME FOR THE MANAGEMENT OF THE SHIRDI SANSTHAN OF SHRI SAI BABA.

1. All the Sansthan property both moveable and immoveable shall vest in the following five trustees for life :—

1. Mr. Moreshwer Vishvanath Pradhan, B. A. LL. B., Member Bombay Legislative Council.

2. Mr. Lakshman Ganesh Mahajani of Messrs. Shoorji Vallabhdas and Co., Merchants Bombay,

3. Prof. Ganesh Govind Narke. Professor of Chemistry and Geology, College of Science, Poona;

4. Ramchandra Atmaram Turkhud, Manager and Secretary, Khatau Makanji Mills, Bombay.

5. Mr. Tatya Ganapati Patil Kote, Land-holder, of Shirdi.

Any vacancy in the trustees shall be filled up by the rest of them as early as possible from among the Bhaktas of Shri Sai Baba subject to confirmation by the District Judge.

2. The management of the Sansthan and its Property both moveable and immoveable shall vest in a Committee called The Shirdi Sansthan Committee, of which the trustees shall be ex-officio members.

3. The Shirdi Sansthan Committee shall consist of 15 members in all, including the trustees and a Chairman, a Treasurer, a Secretary, a Joint Treasurer and a Joint Secretary.

Their names are as follows:—

COMMITTEE.

5. Trustees as in rule 1 above.

CHAIRMAN.

6. Ganesh Dattatraya Sahasrabudhe alias Das Ganu Religious Preceptor and Hardas.

TREASURER.

7. Mr. Govind Rhgunath Dabholkar, Retired Mamlatdar and Resident Magistate (First Class) Bandra.

6

JOINT TREASURER.

8. Mr. Yeshwant Janardan Galwankar, B. A., Judicial
Department, Secretariat, Bombay

SECRETARY.

9. Mr. Hari Sitaram Dikshit, Retired Solicitor and
Vakil High Court,

JOINT SECRETARY.

10. Ramchandra Dada Kote Patil, Land holder of
Shirdi.

MEMBERS.

11. Mr. Krishnarao Narayan Parulkar Honorary
Magistrate, Harda, C. P.

12. Mr. Ganesh Damodar Kelkar, Retired Government servant now residing at Shirdi.

13. Mr. Amaidas B. Mehta, Proprietor, British Photo
Enlarging Company, Kalbadevi, Bombay,

14. Mr. Madhavrao Balwant Deshpande, landholder,
Shirdi. and

15. Mr. Raghuvir Bhaskar Purandare, clerk, Loco
Department G. I P. Ry. Bombay.

4. The above persons (except the trustees who shall
hold office for life) shall hold office for a period of three
years after which all the office holders except trustees shall
be elected by the Bhakta Mandal which shall be constituted
with all convenient despatch in manner hereinafter mentioned

5. The Bhakta Mandal shall consist of such devotees of
Shri Sai Baba's Shrine as apply to be enrolled as members
of the Bhakta Mandal and agree to contribute to the
expenses of the Sansthan a sum not less than Rs 5., per
year. The Shirdi Sansthan Committee however shall have
power for special reasons to be recorded in wrting to enlist
any devotee of the said shrine as an honorary member of the
Bhakta Mandal without requiring him to pay the aforesaid
annual contribution or to make an application as aforesaid.

7

6. The quorum for meetings of the Bhakta Mandal shall be ten members and for that of the Shirdi Sansthan Committee shall be five members.

7. Casual vacancies arising in the Shirdi Sansthan Committee (hereinafter for brevity's sake called the Committee) by death, resignation or otherwise shall be filled up by the Committee.

8. It shall be the duty of the Committee to arrange,

(a) for the management of the Sansthan in accordance with the existing practice but subject to such directions as may from time to time be given by the Bhakta Mandal (hereinafter for brevity's sake called 'Mandal').

(b) for the custody of all cash, documents, papers and other property moveable and immoveable of the Sansthan and for the collection of donations, subscriptions, grants etc., to the Sansthan and for the recovery of the outstandings, rents, profits or other income of the Sansthan and for the payment of all dues, salaries, debts and other reasonable expenses connected with the Sansthan.

(c) for the keeping of true and proper accounts of all things and moneys received and disbursed for or on account of the Sansthan and for the auditing of the same as also for the preparation of the annual balance sheet of the Sansthan and submitting such balance sheet to the Mandal at its annual meeting and a copy of such balance sheet to the District Court of Ahmednagar.

(d) For the holding of the fairs and festivals connected with the Sansthan and for the due entertainment of Puraniks, Kathekaris and Bhajankaris, Singers and mendicants visiting the shrine.

8

(e) for the investment of the surplus funds of the Sansthan or land or such other securities as are mentioned in section 20 of the Indian Trust Act.

(f) for the maintenance in a state of repair of the moveable aud immoveable property of the Sansthan.

9. The Committee shall not have power to alienate, mortgage or charge any immoveable property or jewellery of the Sansthan without the sanction of the District Court of Ahmednagar. It shall however have power to dispose of any other moveable property of the Sansthan or to destroy such articles as may have become useless and unsaleable. It shall have also power to let any immoveable property of the Sansthan at such rental and on such terms as the Committee may think fit but not for a period exceeding three years.

10. The Committee shall as soon as practicable draw up rules not inconsistent with the provisions of this scheme for the following purposes.

(a) formation of the Bhakta Mandal.

(b) holding meetings of the Bhakta Mandal and of the Committee.

(c) for the internal working of the Committee and for the appointment of a local Sub-committee.

(d) generally for the management of the affairs of the Sansthan.

11. The Committee shall have liberty to apply to the District Court for directions whenever it may become necessary or advisable to do so.

Map of Shirdi

Map of Shirdi and neighbouring cities mentioned in this book (artistic impression)

Glossary of Hindi Terms

1. **Adhelis** - Indian currency unit, equal to eight annas or half a rupee.
2. **Agnihotri** - Brahmins who maintain the sacred fire during rituals.
3. **Akshay Tritiya** - also known as Akti or Akha Teej, is a festival celebrating annual springtime, observed by Hindus and Jains in April or May.
4. **Annachatra(s)** - free-food distribution centres.
5. **Arpan** - offering.
6. **Ashtak** - a form of poetry in eight stanzas.
7. **Ashwin Shudh/Shukl** - the seventh month of the Hindu Calendar, which overlaps in the Gregorian months of September and October.
8. **Bairagi** - a recluse.
9. **Bhadrapad** - is the sixth month of the Hindu calendar, between August-September.
10. **Bhakri** - a flat, round and unleavened bread.
11. **Bhiksha** - alms.
12. **Bodh vachans** - words of wisdom or awakening.
13. **Brahma gyan** - the knowledge about the Creator.
14. **Central Provinces** - was an administrative division containing the present states of Madhya Pradesh, Chhattisgarh and Maharashtra, with Nagpur as the capital.
15. **Chaitra** - the first month of the year in the Hindu calendar, which falls between March-April.
16. **Chamara** - a hand fan.
17. **Chaulis** - old Indian currency which was 3/4th of a rupee.
18. **Chawadi** - an assembly place open from four sides, in a village.
19. **Chhata/Chatri** - an umbrella.

20. **Chitnis** - secretary.
21. **Dakshina** - any kind of donation given to a teacher, temple, priest or saint. It can also be in the form of charity or giving of alms.
22. **Dalaan** - verandah.
23. **Dalals** - a broker or agent.
24. **Dattajayanti or Dattatreya Jayanti** - a Hindu festival which celebrates the birth of Lord Dattatreya, said to be the incarnation of Lord Brahma, Vishnu and Mahesh. It falls on the full-moon day between December and January.
25. **Daya-Moorty** - the idol of mercy.
26. **Deccani Urdu** - a language that was used in the Sultanates in the Deccan region and is somewhat similar to Urdu.
27. **Devalaya(s)** - a temple or shrine.
28. **Dharma rahasya** - the mystery of life which is revealed by religion.
29. **Dhuni** - the sacred fire which was kept burning by Sai Baba in Dwarkamayi. The Udi is produced from here.
30. **Diwan-khana** - A common hall.
31. **Durbar mandal** - An organization or council of workers.
32. **Dussehra/Vijayadashami** - a major Hindu festival celebrated at the end of Navratri, which falls in the month of September or October. It signifies the victory of good over evil.
33. **Dwarkamayi** - a pilgrimage site in Shirdi, which was once an old dilapidated mosque where Sai Baba stayed and met his devotees till the end of his life.
34. **Ekadasi** - it is the eleventh day of each half of the month in the Hindu calendar. There are two Ekadasi days in each month.
35. **Ekanta dhyana** - meditation in solitude.
36. **Eknathi Bhagawat** - a commentary on the *Bhagawat Puran* of Lord Krishna in Marathi by Saint Eknath.
37. **Guntha** - measure of area, equaling to 101.2 square metres.
38. **Guru Purnima** - a Hindu festival that is celebrated to honour and worship the guru or spiritual teacher. It falls on the full-moon day in the months of June or July.

39. **Gurusthan** - place of the guru or the master. It is the place under the neem tree in Shirdi which Sai Baba used to call his guru's place.
40. **Jhaari** - jug.
41. **Jnaneshwari** - an interpretation of the Bhagavad Gita in Marathi language by Saint Jnanadev.
42. **Jyeshtha** - the third month in the Hindu calendar, falls between May and June.
43. **Kafni** - a long robe worn by Sai Baba.
44. **Kartik month** - the eighth month of the Hindu calendar, falls between October and November.
45. **Karyakari mandal** - a group of workers.
46. **Kathakar** - a storyteller.
47. **Kesari** - a newspaper in Marathi, first published by Lokmanya Bal Gangadhar Tilak in 1881 from Pune, Maharashtra.
48. **Khandoba Mandir** - a temple in Shirdi dedicated to Lord Khandoba, who is believed to be the manifestation of Lord Shiva.
49. **Kirtankars** - a group of singers who sing devotional songs, while narrating the divine attributes of God or a saint.
50. **Kudaal** - a hoe.
51. **Lac/Lakh** - in the Indian number system, one lakh is equal to one hundred thousand.
52. **Leela(s)** - divine activities.
53. **Lendibagh** - the land adjoining the narrow streamlet in the outskirts of the village.
54. **Lendi** - land which was used as a toilet.
55. **Mahasamadhi** - the act of consciously leaving one's human body, undertaken by a realized Yogi or Yogini (practitioners of meditation).
56. **Mamlatdar** - a government official responsible for the collection of revenue.
57. **Mandali** - group of people.
58. **Mangalacharan** - invocation of the deity before starting a work.
59. **Mankari(s)** - a title used by Maratha nobility.
60. **Mantra shakti** - power of the hymns.

61. **Mauli** - mother (in Marathi).
62. **Modi script** - a script used to write Marathi language.
63. **Morchal** - A hand-fan made of peacock feathers.
64. **Murlidhar** - the idol of Lord Krishna playing the flute.
65. **Naib Diwan** - Deputy Chief Treasurer/Official.
66. **Naivedya** - an offering to God, usually food.
67. **Nandi** - the bull functioning as the gate-guardian of Lord Shiva at Kailash.
68. **Niryan** - Mahasamadhi.
69. **Nitya niyamas** - Daily practices or activities.
70. **Ovi** - a stanza of a particular measure.
71. **Padukas** - footwear.
72. **Palki** - a palanquin.
73. **Pan beeda** - a preparation combining betel leaf with areca nut.
74. **Panchnama** - document signed by five elected members of the village council.
75. **Paramarthic** - actions/rituals made before leaving the human body.
76. **Parayan** - complete reading of a holy scripture.
77. **Patil** - headman of a village.
78. **Patka** - a man's head-covering consisting of a small piece of cloth wrapped around his head.
79. **Patrika** - magazine.
80. **Peer/Pir** - a saint.
81. **Pies** - a small unit of currency in India till 1957, which was equal to 1/12 of a rupee.
82. **Pindarpan** - sacrificial rites in the memory of a deceased person.
83. **Pothi** - a religious manuscript or scripture.
84. **Pouvlis** - Indian currency which equals twenty-five paise.
85. **Prabhu** - God.
86. **Pradakshina** - the action of walking clockwise around a person or deity as a mark of respect.
87. **Prasadalaya** - a place where food is served after it is offered to God.
88. **Punyatithi** - death anniversary.

89. **Purnima** - full-moon day.
90. **Pushpak viman** - an air borne chariot.
91. **Ramayan** - a Hindu epic on Lord Ram attributed to Valmiki, a Hindu saint.
92. **Ramnavami festival** - a Hindu festival in which Lord Rama's birth is celebrated. It falls in the month of March or April every year.
93. **Ram Vijaya** - a holy and revered book of Hindu religion which is read by the devotees of Lord Ram, especially during Vijayadashami.
94. **Rath** - chariot.
95. **Rinanubandha** - past-life karmic ties.
96. **Sabha mandap** - a meeting or assembly building, traditionally where local issues are discussed.
97. **Sadgati** - liberation from the cycle of birth and death.
98. **Sadguru** - spiritual master.
99. **Sainath Prabha** - the first magazine published during Sai Baba's time from Shirdi by Dakshina Bhiksha Sanstha, from 1916 to 1919.
100. **Sai Sagunopasna** - a book by K.J. Bhishma which contained, besides the aarti-psalms composed on Sai Baba, some traditional hymns from the Hindu liturgy written by various writers.
101. **Samadhi Mandir** - formerly the Buti wada, it is the temple and shrine of Sai Baba.
102. **Samartha** - spiritually capable.
103. **Satka** - a short wooden stick used by Sai Baba.
104. **Seeda** - the practice of donating uncooked food.
105. **Seemolangan** - crossing over the ocean of worldly life.
106. **Sevakari** - a worker; one devoted to serve the Guru or the deity.
107. **Shishya** - disciple.
108. **Shiv Pindi** - Lord Siva represented as a phallic symbol, sitting on a disc-shaped platform.
109. **Shloka** - verses in Sanskrit that originated from Vedas.
110. **Shravan** - it is the fifth month in the Hindu calendar, falls between July and August.

111. **Shri Saibaba Sansthan Trust, Shirdi** - established in 1922, it is the governing and administrative body of Sai Baba's Samadhi and all other temples in the premises. It also works towards the development of the Shirdi village.

112. **Shri Sai Leela** - the first official magazine published by the Shri Saibaba Sansthan Trust, Shirdi in 1923.

113. **Shri Sainath mahima strotram** - verses written on Sai Baba by Upasani Maharaj.

114. **Shri Sai Satcharita** - written by Govind Raghunath Dabholkar alias Hemadpant, it is a biographical book based on the life and teachings of Sai Baba. It was originally written in Marathi and was published in 1930 by the Shri Saibaba Sansthan, Shirdi. It has been translated into many other languages.

115. **Shri Geeta** - also known as the Bhagavad Gita, it is a Hindu scripture which is a part of the epic of Mahabharata written by Vyasa, in Sanskrit.

116. **Sthapna** - installation.

117. **Tamashawala** - an entertainer or a village showman.

118. **Tilanjali/Tiltarpan** - a ceremony in the honour of the ancestors in which an oblation of a handful of water and sesame seed is made to the deceased.

119. **Trishul** - a trident.

120. **Turbat** - a tomb.

121. **Udi** - also known as vibhuti or bhasam, is a term for the sacred ash produced by burning dried wood.

122. **Upadesh** - a discourse or instruction.

123. **Vijayadashami** - same as Dussehra.

124. **Vyas Peeth** - a significant place/platform/stage in the temple.

125. **Wada** - a residential accommodation.

126. **Yoga Vasistha** - a book on the discourse imparted by Sage Vasistha to Lord Ram, written by Valmiki.

Glossary of Names

1. **Abdul** - a devotee of Sai Baba from Nanded, Maharashtra who first came to visit Shirdi in 1889. He used to read the Quran while sitting with Baba, who used to quote some lines from this holy scripture. He recorded some of the statements of Sai Baba in Marathi / Modi language in Urdu alphabets.

2. **Abdullah Jan** - Pathan, Muhammadan, was born in 1896 in Tarbella, Pakistan but lived at Korhale, near Sakori in Ahmednagar district, Maharashtra. He met Sai Baba in 1913 and became his devotee.

3. **Abdul Rahim** - alias Abdul Rahim Shamsuddin Rangari, a Muslim devotee, who lived in Thane, Maharashtra and first met Sai Baba in 1913.

4. **Acharya Ekkirala Bhardwaja** - authored many books on Hindu spiritualism, predominantly on Sai Baba and Dattatreya.

5. **Akkalkot Maharaj** - alias Swami Samarth, believed to be an incarnation of Lord Dattatreya, stayed in Akkalkot in Solapur District of Maharashtra for about twenty-two years, until his Samadhi in 1878.

6. **Amir Shakkar** - a Muslim devotee of Sai Baba who was from village Korhla in Kopargaon District. He worked as a commission agent in Bandra.

7. **Anna Chinchinkar** - alias Damodar Ghanashyam Babare, was a devotee of Sai Baba who hailed from Chinchani village in Thane district of Maharashtra. He renovated the Chawadi in Shirdi in Shaka 1859.

8. **Appa Jagale** - a friend of Mhalsapati who, along with Shimpi, provided food to the saints and devoted souls who came to Shirdi.

9. **B.V. Dev** - a Mamlatdar in Dhanu town of Maharashtra, who wrote several articles in the *Shri Sai Leela* magazine. He also prepared the index of the *Shri Sai Satcharita*.

10. **Bade Baba** - alias Murabe Mehrban Pir Muhamad, Fakir Baba or Mote Baba, was a devotee of Sai Baba from Malegaon in Nasik district of Maharashtra, India. He first visited Shirdi in around 1909. Being a close devotee of Sai Baba, he received dakshina from him on a daily basis.

11. **Bahadur Shah Zafar** - was the last Mughal emperor of India.

12. **Baijabai Kote Patil** - wife of Ganpati Kote Patil and mother of Tatya Kote Patil, used to feed Sai Baba before he moved into Dwarkamayi and, later, used to give alms to him when he approached her doorstep each day.

13. **Balabhau Chandorkar** - a nephew of Nanasaheb Chandorkar, he owned a small hotel in Shirdi during Sai Baba's time.

14. **Balaji Vasant Talim** - was a prominent sculptor who sculpted Sai Baba's statue. The statue was installed in 1954 in the Samadhi Mandir and is worshipped daily since then.

15. **Balkrishna Khaparde** - alias Balasaheb Khaparde, son of G.S. Khaparde, was an eminent lawyer from Amraoti. He was the leader of the Swaraj Party and a Minister of the Central Provinces and Berar.

16. **Balasaheb Bhate** - alias Purushottam Sakharam Bhate, was the Mamlatdar at Kopargaon from 1904 to 1909. He visited Sai Baba in Shirdi in 1894-95 and later decided to settle there permanently.

17. **Bal Gangadhar Tilak** - alias Lokmanya Tilak or "Father of the Indian Unrest", was an Indian nationalist, political activist, social reformer and the leader of the extremists group, who played an eminent role in the Indian Independence Movement.

18. **Balakrishna Shivram Munje** - was a political activist, social reformer, freedom fighter and a supporter of Bal Gangadhar Tilak. He also served as the General Secretary of Central Indian Provincial Congress upto 1920.

19. **Banne Mia Fakir** - a Sufi ascetic from Aurangabad.

20. **Bappaji Laxmanrao Ratnaparkhi** - a resident of Shirdi, who was the maternal uncle of Shama.

21. **Bayaji Appa Kote Patil** - was the revenue or the Police Patil of Birgaon, who owned large acres of land. Sai Baba used to take alms from his house daily.

22. **Bhagoji Shinde** - a local devotee of Sai Baba who suffered from leprosy and served him till his Mahasamadhi.

23. **Bhai Krishnaji Alibagkar** - a devotee of Akkalkot Maharaj who contributed towards the installation of Sai Baba's padukas in Gurusthan in 1912.

24. **Bhaskar Sadashiv Satam** - joined the police force in 1911 and was the sub-inspector of Bombay Police. He visited Shirdi in 1940, after Sai Baba's Mahasamadhi.

25. **Bipin Chandra Pal** - also known as the "Father of Revolutionary Thoughts" was an Indian activist and freedom fighter and a supporter of Bal Gangadhar Tilak. He had great contributions in the Indian Independence movement.

26. **Chand Bhai Patil** - was the headman of Dhupkheda village in Aurangabad district, Maharashtra.

27. **Chitambar Keshav Gadgil** - pensioned Mamlatdar, who was the Secretary and Accountant of the Dakshina Bhiksha Sanstha from 1916 to 1917.

28. **Dada Kelkar** - alias Ganesh Damodar Kelkar was the father-in-law of H.V. Sathe

29. **Dasganu** - Ganpatrao Dattaraya Sahastrabuddhe was the Police Constable of Shrigonda Village in Ahmednagar District. He became an itinerant minstrel or kirtankar, propagating about Sai Baba and his divine personality wherever he went. He wrote books titled *Bhakta Leelamrit, Santa Kathamrit* and *Bhakta Saramrit*. A few pieces of his compositions are incorporated in the aarti of Sai Baba at Shirdi.

30. **Dr. Chidambaram Pillay** - a close devotee of Sai Baba who was addressed as Bhau (brother) by Baba.

31. **Dr. Rajgopal Chari** - a devotee of Sai Baba from Nellore city in Andhra Pradesh.

32. **G.G. Narke** - alias Ganesh Govind Narke, was a Professor of Geology and Chemistry in the College of Engineering, Pune and the son-in-law of Bapusaheb Buti. He first visited Baba in 1913 and became a Trustee in charge of the Buti wada.

33. **G.S. Khaparde** - was a prominent lawyer, a political activist from Amravati and a close associate of Lokmanya Bal Gangadhar

Tilak. He became an ardent devotee of Sai Baba and diarized his five visits to Shirdi.

34. **Ganesh Vishnu Behere** - was a devotee of Sai Baba.

35. **Ganpati Kote Patil** - a landlord in Shirdi, who was the husband of Baijabai and the father of Tatya Kote Patil. Sai Baba used to routinely beg for alms from their house.

36. **Gopalrao Mukund Buti** - alias Bapusaheb Buti, was a rich devotee of Sai Baba from Nagpur, Maharashtra, who constructed the Buti wada. It is now known as the Samadhi Temple of Sai Baba.

37. **Govind Raghunath Dabholkar** - alias Hemadpant, author of the famous *Shri Sai Satcharita: The Wonderful Life and Teachings of Shri Sai Baba*. He was from Thane district in Maharashtra. He was the Resident Magistrate first class, at Bandra, from 1903 to 1907 and paid his first visit to Shirdi in 1910.

38. **H.A. Damson** - was a member of the Council of the Governor-General of India.

39. **Harish Balaji Talim** - the son of Late Balaji Vasant Talim, who sculpted the idol of Sai Baba for the Gurusthan.

40. **Hari Sitaram Dixit** - also known as Kakasaheb Dixit or Kaka, was an eminent lawyer and a solicitor from Mumbai who first visited Sai Baba on 2nd November 1909. He built the Dixit wada in Shirdi. He was also instrumental in the establishment and working of the Shri Saibaba Sansthan Trust, Shirdi in 1926 and became its Honorary Secretary. He also looked after the *Shri Sai Leela*, the monthly Marathi magazine published by the Sansthan.

41. **Harold A. Stuart** - was the first Director of the Central Criminal Intelligence Department in India and later became the Home Secretary.

42. **Imam Bhai Chote Khan** - a resident of Vaijapur, Aurangabad, was the Nizam's sepoy in the Mamlatdar Office who heard about Sai Baba in 1910.

43. **Jyotindra Tarkhad** - was the youngest son of R.A. Tarkhad.

44. **Kashinath Govindrao alias Upasani Maharaj** - also known as Upasani Shastri, was a disciple of Sai Baba who lived in Sakori, a place 5.7 km away from Shirdi, in his ashram.

45. **Kashinath Kanderao Garde** - was a retired Sub-Judge of Nagpur and a devotee of Sai Baba.

46. **Kashiram Bala Shimpi** - a local tailor, who looked after the saints and ascetic visitors of Sai Baba at Shirdi. He used to serve Baba and provided wood for the Dhuni in Dwarkamayi.

47. **Krishna Shastri Jogeshwar Bhishma** - from village Butibori in Nagpur District of Maharashtra, India, was a Revenue Inspector. He prepared a booklet titled *Sai Sagunopasana* which contained, besides the aarti and psalms sung to Sai Baba, some hymns from the Hindu liturgy.

48. **Khushal Chand** - a devotee of Sai Baba who belonged to the Marwari community and stayed in village Rahata.

49. **Laxman Bhatt Joshi** - a local devotee of Sai Baba of Shirdi.

50. **Laxmi Bai** - alias Laxmibai Tukaram Shinde, originally from Yeola village in Nasik District of Maharashtra. She was married in the Shinde family. Before Sai Baba took Mahasamadhi, he gave nine coins to her which are believed to represent the nine forms of devotion.

51. **Laxman Ganesh Mahajani** - alias Kaka Mahajani, was the editor of *Shri Sai Leela* magazine for some time.

52. **Laxman Krishnaji Noolkar alias Tatya Saheb Noolkar** - was a Judge in Pandharpur town of Maharashtra, who first visited Sai Baba in 1909 and he had the good fortune of the first worship of Sai Baba.

53. **Laxmibai Khaparde** - addressed as Ajibai by Sai Baba, was the wife of Ganesh Shrikrishna Khaparde, who was devoted to Sai Baba and used to carry food personally for him to Dwarkamayi.

54. **Lord Curzon** - George Nathaniel Curzon was the Viceroy of India from 1899 to 1905.

55. **Lord Gilbert Elliot-Minto** - alias Gilbert Elliot-Murray-Kynynmound fourth Earl of Minto, was a British aristocrat and politician who served as the seventeenth Viceroy and Governor-General of India from 1905 to 1910.

56. **Lt. Col. M.B. Nimbalkar** - was from Vadodra, Gujarat. A graduate in English and Marathi literature, he wrote articles in *Shri Sai Leela* magazine and authored the book *Shri Sai Baba's Teaching and Philosophies*.

57. **Madhavrao Deshpande alias Shama** - was an ardent devotee of Sai Baba, who was born in Nimon village in Sangamner district of Maharashtra. He moved to Shirdi when he was 2 to 3 years old. He studied upto sixth standard in Shirdi and became the assistant teacher in the local school.

58. **Meghashyam Balwant Rege** - Judge of the Indore High Court who was an ardent devotee of Sai Baba.

59. **Megha** - the cook of H.V. Sathe, who was a devotee of Lord Shiva and Sai Baba. He performed the daily aarti of Sai Baba at Dwarkamayi and Chawadi.

60. **Mhalsapati Chimnaji Nagare** - a resident of Shirdi and the priest of the Khandoba temple, who was a close devotee of Sai Baba. When he saw the Fakir Sai Baba for the first time, he cried out "Aao Sai" meaning "Come Sai". After that the Fakir came to be known as Sai Baba.

61. **Mohandas Karamchand Gandhi** - also known as "Bapu" and "Mahatma Gandhi", is said to have brought India independence from the British rule through a non-violent civil disobedience movement. He inspired non-violent movements for civil rights and freedom across the world.

62. **Moreshwar W. Pradhan** - was a pleader in the Bombay High Court and Justice of Peace, who first visited Shirdi in 1910 for some time. He was among the first five trustees of the Sansthan. In 1913, he hired a famous painter, Shamrao Jaykar, to paint Sai Baba's portrait and in 1933 he published a book in English *Shri Sai Baba of Shirdi – A Glimpse of Indian Spirituality* which dealt with the life and teachings of Sai Baba.

63. **Mr. Natekar** - a spy deployed by the British Government for keeping an eye of G.S. Khaparde, who was known as Hamsa for he wore the attire of a sadhu for his job.

64. **Muktaram** - visited Shirdi around 1910-1911 from Raver, District Jalgaon of Maharashtra

65. **Nagesh Atmaram Sawant** - was the sub-inspector of the Bombay City Police who visited Shirdi after Sai Baba's Mahasamadhi.

66. **Nanasaheb Nimonkar** - alias Shankarrao Raghunath Deshpande, was a devotee of Sai Baba from Nimon, a village

20 miles away from Shirdi. He was a Special Magistrate of Sangamner.

67. **Narayan Govind Chandorkar** - popularly called Nana or Nanasaheb, was an ardent devotee of Sai Baba from Kalyan, Mumbai, who first visited Shirdi in 1892. He was a Deputy Collector and was responsible for spreading Sai Baba's name far-and-wide.

68. **P.J. Mead** - the Collector of Ahmednagar District, Maharashtra.

69. **R.H. Craddock** - Chief Commissioner of the Central Provinces in 1909.

70. **Ramkrishna Shrikrishna Navalkar** - a devotee of Sai Baba who bought the Sathe wada in 1924 and later gave it to Shri Saibaba Sansthan Trust, Shirdi in 1939.

71. **Radhakrishna Ayi** - alias Sunderabai Ksheersagar was a widow from Ahmednagar, who visited Sai Baba in 1905 and thereafter spent her whole life at Shirdi, serving him. She was one of the persons who looked after the various arrangements for Sai Baba and his devotees, including provision of food.

72. **Raghuji Ganpat Scindia Patel** - was a landowner and a retired revenue Patil from Shirdi who was a staunch devotee of Sai Baba.

73. **Raghunathrao Tendulkar** - husband of Savitribai Tendulkar, from Bandra, Mumbai, who was the author of *Shri Sainath Bhajanmala*.

74. **Raghuvir Bhaskar Purandhare** - a devotee of Sai Baba who worked as a clerk in the Railway Department at Bandra and first visited Sai Baba in 1909. Later, he worked as the Joint Treasurer of the Shri Saibaba Sansthan Trust, Shirdi.

75. **Ramachandra Atmaram Tarkhad (R.A. Tarkhad)** - alias Babasaheb Tarkhad, was the Manager and Secretary in the well-known Khatau Mills in Bombay. He was a rich and influential devotee of Sai Baba and published *Shri Sai Satcharita* in 1930.

76. **Ramachandra Dada Kote Patil** - a resident of Shirdi, who was a close friend of Tatya Kote Patil and a staunch devotee of Sai Baba.

77. **Ramadas Bidkar Maharaj** - was a disciple of Shri Akkalkot Maharaj and had established a hermitage in Pune city of Maharashtra.

78. **Ramgir Bua** - was a resident of Shirdi and a disciple of Gangagir of Sada. He was in Shirdi at his grandmother's house when Sai Baba first arrived in Shirdi.

79. **Ramrao Kothare** - was a medical doctor from Bombay who came to Shirdi in 1912. He had sent marble padukas for the Gurusthan.

80. **Rao Bahadur Hari Vinayak Sathe** - was a devotee of Sai Baba who was the Deputy Collector in the Ahmednagar District of Maharashtra. He first visited Sai Baba in 1904 and rendered yeoman service to him.

81. **S.B. Dhumal** - was a pleader in Nasik, Maharashtra.

82. **Sagun Meru Naik** - came from Pune to Shirdi in 1911-12, where he started running a tea shop with refreshments and also sold items like Sai Baba's pictures, aarti books and other general items used in a worship.

83. **Sakharam Hari Jog** - alias Bapusaheb Jog came to Shirdi in 1906, after retiring from the Public Works Department in Pune. He conducted the daily worship of Sai Baba in Dwarkamayi and Chawadi thrice a day after Megha's death in 1912 and continued this till Sai Baba's Mahasamadhi. After Sai Baba's Mahasamadhi, Bapusaheb along with Upasani Maharaj went to Prayagraj in Uttar Pradesh to carry out the funeral rites of Sai Baba.

84. **Sakharam Mahadu Patil Kote** - was a wealthy landlord and devotee from Shirdi.

85. **Savitribai Tendulkar** - was the wife of Raghunathrao Tendulkar of Bandra, Mumbai. She was an ardent devotee of Sai Baba and wrote several articles in *Shri Sai Leela* magazine. She co-authored the famous book *Shri Sainath Bhajanmala* with her husband.

86. **Shamrao Jaykar** - a resident of Mumbai and a renowned painter who used to paint portraits of the British Lords or people belonging to the royal families. He first visited Shirdi in 1913 and painted four portraits of Sai Baba.

87. **Shamsuddin Mia** - a Sufi ascetic from Aurangabad.

88. **Shankar Narayan Joshi** - alias Nanavali, was an ardent devotee of Sai Baba, who passed away on the thirteenth day of Sai Baba's Mahasamadhi, that is, 27th October 1918.

89. **Tatya Kote Patil** - was the son of Ganapati Kote Patil and Baiyja Kote Patil. He was an ardent devotee of Sai Baba. He received a large amount of money from Sai Baba on a daily basis.

90. **Vamanrao Patel alias Swami Sharananand** - was an ardent devotee of Sai Baba who wrote *Gurusmriti* and *Sai Baba*, in Gujarati. In 1961, he wrote the book *Sai Baba the Superman* in English.

91. **Yashwantrao D. Dave** - was a devotee from Mumbai who donated Sai Baba's idol, of about 3 ft height, which was kept in Gurusthan.

Bibliography

Aher, Pramod (2017). *Shirdi Gazetteer: Untold Stories.* Shirdi: Yugandhar Prakashan

Ambekar, Shrikant Ganesh (1997). *Sai Sagrateel 88 Moti.* Pune: Aatmajyot Prakashan

Bhardwaja, Acharya E. (1993). *Sai Baba: The Master.* Ongole, Andhra Pradesh: Sri Gurupaduka Publications

Chitluri, Vinny (2000). *Ambrosia in Shirdi.* Bangalore: Shirdi Sai Baba Satsang

Chitluri, Vinny (2009, 2012). *Baba's Gurukul: Shirdi.* New Delhi: Sterling Publishers Pvt. Ltd.

Dabholkar, Govind Raghunath (1930). *Shri Sai Satcharita: The Wonderful Life and Teachings of Shri Sai Baba.* Translated from Marathi to English by Gunaji, N.V. (2002). Shirdi: Shri Saibaba Sansthan Trust, Shirdi

Dabholkar, Govind R. (1930). *Shri Sai Satcharita: The Life and Teachings of Shirdi Sai Baba.* Translated from Marathi to English by Indira Kher (1999, 2013, 2014, 2015). New Delhi: Sterling Publishers Pvt. Ltd.

Dikshit, Vishnu Prasad (undated). *Upasani Ratnayam.* Hyderabad: Printer Marwari Press Afzalganj

Gokhale, V.R. (2004). *Nirvanicha Sakha.* Mumbai: Nemi Chand H. Shah

Kamath, M.V. and V.B. Kher (1995). *Sai Baba of Shirdi: A Unique Saint.* Mumbai: Jaico Publishing House

Kavade, Pandurang Balaji (1956). *Shri Kshetra Shirdiche Mahan Sant Shri Sai Maharaj Yanche Charitra.* Nasik: Dattatray Shankar Potnis, Gaokari Press

Khaparde, Balkrishna Ganesh (1962). *Dada Saheb Khaparde Yanche Charitra.* Pune: Y.G. Joshi. Prasad Prakashan

Khaparde, G.S. (undated). *Shirdi Diary of Honorable Mr. G.S. Khaparde.* Shirdi: Shri Saibaba Sansthan Trust, Shirdi

Kher, V.B. (2001, 2004, 2008, 2016). *Sai Baba: His Divine Glimpses.* New Delhi: Sterling Publishers Pvt. Ltd.

McLain, Karline (2016). *The Afterlife of Sai Baba: Competing Visions of a Global Saint.* New Delhi: Orient Blackswan Pvt. Ltd.

Nayar, Pramod K. (2007). *The Trial of Bahadur Shah Zafar.* Hyderabad: Orient Blackswan Pvt. Ltd.

Newton, A.P. (1940). *A Hundred Years of The British Empire,* London: Duckworth.

Nimbalkar, M.B. (2002, 2004). *Shri Sai Baba's Teachings & Philosophy.* New Delhi: Sterling Publishers Pvt. Ltd.

Osborne, Arthur (1972). *The Incredible Sai Baba: The Life and Miracles of a Modern-day Saint.* Mumbai: Orient Longman India

Pradhan, M.W. (1933, 1943). *Shri Saibaba of Shirdi: A Glimpse of Indian Spirituality.* Shirdi: R.A Turkhud, Bandra

Rigopoulos, Antonio (1993). *The Life & Teachings of Sai Baba of Shirdi.* Delhi: Sri Satguru Publications

Sharananad, Sai (1983). *Sai Natha Ne Sharne.* Mumbai: Madhusudan Bhatt

Shepherd, Kevin R.D. (2015). *Sai Baba of Shirdi: A Biographical Investigation.* New Delhi: Sterling Publishers Pvt. Ltd.

Shepherd, Kevin R.D. (2017). *Sai Baba: Faqir of Shirdi.* New Delhi: Sterling Publishers Pvt. Ltd.

Swami, B.V. Narasimha (1994). *Life of Sai Baba* (4 volumes). Chennai: All India Sai Samaj

Swami, B.V. Narasimha (2004). *Life of Sai Baba* (combined). Chennai: All India Sai Samaj

Swami, B.V. Narasimha (2005). *Sri Sai Baba's Charters & Sayings.* Chennai: All India Sai Samaj

Swami, B.V. Narasimha (2006). *Devotees' Experiences of Sai Baba.* Part I, II, III and IV. Chennai: All India Sai Samaj

Warren, Marianne (2011). *Unravelling the Enigma: Shirdi Sai Baba in the Light of Sufism.* New Delhi: Sterling Publishers Pvt. Ltd.

Williams, Alison (2002, 2004). *Experiencing Sai Baba's Shirdi: A Guide.* Shirdi: Saipatham Publications

e-Books

Dixit, Kakasaheb (undated). *The Diary of Kakasaheb Dixit.* 7dagenshirdisai.nl/de-content/uploads/2012/01/kakasaheb-dixits-diary1.pdf. Accessed on 26 September 2018

Pradhan, Rao Bahadur M.W. (1933). *Shri Sai Baba of Shirdi: A Glimpse of Indian Spirituality.*
saileelas.org/books/spirituality.htm. Accessed on 26 September 2018

Websites/Weblinks

abhilekh-patal.in/jspui

online.sai.org.in

shirdisaibabamahasamadhi.blogspot.com/2018/11 mahasamadhi-
babas-death-certificate.html

Journals and Magazines

Mahajani, Laxman Ganesh Shaka 1845 (1923). *Shri Sai Leela*. Bandra:
Tarkhad, Ramchandra Atmaram

Mahajani, Laxman Ganesh Shaka 1846 (1924). *Shri Sai Leela*. Bandra:
Tarkhad, Ramchandra Atmaram

Mahajani, Laxman Ganesh Shaka 1847 (1925). *Shri Sai Leela*. Bandra:
Tarkhad, Ramchandra Atmaram

Mahajani, Laxman Ganesh Shaka 1848 (1926). *Shri Sai Leela*. Bandra:
Tarkhad, Ramchandra Atmaram

Mahajani, Laxman Ganesh Shaka 1849 (1927). *Shri Sai Leela*. Bandra:
Tarkhad, Ramchandra Atmaram

Tarkhad, Ramchandra Atmaram Shaka 1853 (1931). *Shri Sai Leela*.
Bandra: Tarkhad, Ramchandra Atmaram

Tarkhad, Ramchandra Atmaram Shaka 1854 (1932). *Shri Sai Leela*.
Bandra: Tarkhad, Ramchandra Atmaram

Tarkhad, Ramchandra Atmaram Shaka 1855 (1933). *Shri Sai Leela*.
Bandra: Tarkhad, Ramchandra Atmaram

Tarkhad, Ramchandra Atmaram Shaka 1856 (1934). *Shri Sai Leela*.
Bandra: Tarkhad, Ramchandra Atmaram

Tarkhad, Ramchandra Atmaram Shaka 1857 (1935). *Shri Sai Leela*.
Bandra: Tarkhad, Ramchandra Atmaram

Nawalkar, Sundar Rao Shaka 1858 (1936). *Shri Sai Leela*. Mumbai: Shri
Saileela, Princess Street

Samant, Ramchandra Ramkrishna Shaka 1859 (1937). *Shri Sai Leela*.
Mumbai: Shri Saileela, Princess Street

Ghaisas, Ramchandra Vasudev Shaka 1861 (1939). *Shri Sai Leela*.
Mumbai: Ghaisas, Ramchandra Vasudev

Ghaisas, Ramchandra Vasudev Shaka 1862 (1940). *Shri Sai Leela*.
Mumbai, Ghaisas, Ramchandra Vasudev

Ghaisas, Ramchandra Vasudev Shaka 1863 (1941). *Shri Sai Leela*.
Mumbai: Ghaisas, Ramchandra Vasudev

Ghaisas, Ramchandra Vasudev (1942). *Shri Sai Leela*. Mumbai: Ghaisas,
Ramchandra Vasudev

Kakre, A.H. (1981). *Shri Sai Leela*. Mumbai

Kakre, A.H. (1983). *Shri Sai Leela*. Mumbai

Banne, R.D. (1984). *Shri Sai Leela*. Mumbai

Tathe, Vidyadhar (2007). *Shri Sai Leela*. Internet edition. www.sai.org.in

Sainath Prabha (1916). Kiran 3 (1917, 1918, 1919), Kiran 1 (1916), Kiran 2 (1916), Kiran 11 (1918), Kiran 5 (1918), Kiran 4 (1917), Kiran 1 January (1919)

Narayan, Naib Diwan Sunderrao (1916). *Shri Sainath Prabha*.Shirdi: Dakshina Bhiksha Sansthan

Petkar, Laxman Balvant (1918). *Shri Sainath Prabha*. Shirdi, Dakshina Bhiksha Sansthan

Petkar, Laxman Balvant (1919). *Shri Sainath Prabha*. Shirdi, Dakshina Bhiksha Sansthan

Government Reports

Government of Maharashtra. Report of Maharashtra Gazetteer 1916

Government of Maharashtra. Birth and Death Register of Kopergaon 1918

Government of Maharashtra. Original Students Attendance Register of the School in Shirdi 1881

Government of India (1911). Weekly Criminal Intelligence Report. Directorate of Criminal Intelligence, Department of Home

Government of India (1912). Weekly Criminal Intelligence Report. Directorate of Criminal Intelligence, Department of Home

Government of India (1909). Report by Mr. C. R. Cleveland, Inspector-General of Police, Central Provinces, on the Proposed Deportation of G. S. Khaparde and Dr. Munje under Regulation III of 1818, Department of Home.

STERLING⊒

BOOKS ON
SHIRDI SAI BABA

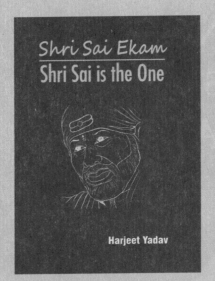

Shri Sai Ekam- Shri Sai is the One

HARJEET YADAV
978 93 86245 38 0
6.75"×9.5"
592pp+16 pages 210 photographs
Paperback ₹ 900

SAI: Thy Spring is Love of My Life

G. K. SOOD
978 93 86245 25 0
4.8"×7.6"
48pp on art paper
Paperback ₹ 75

हमें साई की आवश्यकता है सदा के लिए 6, 16 और 60!

सौरभ खन्ना
978 93 86245 21 2
4.8"×7.6" 88pp
Paperback ₹ 125

श्री साई ज्ञानेश्वरी- महाकाव्य

राकेश जुनेजा
978 93 86245 17 5
5.5"×8.5" 280pp
Hardbound ₹ 250

Shirdi Sai Baba is a household name in India as well as in many parts of the World today. Sterling Publishers are well known for publishing the largest number of books on Shirdi Sai, indeed far more than any other publisher. We endeavour to be comprehensive in the range of author and content. We also publish books on other saints and masters.

SHIRDI
within & beyond
A collection of unseen
& rare photographs
*Dr. Rabinder Nath
Kakarya*
978 81 207 7806 1
₹ 750

Sai Baba: Faqir of Shirdi
Kevin R.D. Shepherd
ISBN 978 93 86245 06 9
₹ 350

Promises of Shirdi Sai Baba
(The Eleven Precious Sayings)
Bela Sharma
ISBN 978 93 85913 98 3
₹ 75

Shri Sai Gyaneshwari
Rakesh Juneja
ISBN 978 93 86245 05 2
₹ 300

Shirdi Sai Baba
Anusuya Vasudevan
ISBN 978 93 86245 16 8
(64 pages plates)
₹ 200

We need Sai forever... at 6, 16 and 60!
Saurabh Khanna
ISBN 978 93 86245 15 1
₹ 190

Sai Baba of Shirdi:
A Biographical Investigation
Kevin R. D. Shepherd
ISBN 978 81 207 9901 1
₹450

The Eternal Sai
Consciousness
A. R. Nanda
ISBN 978 81 207 9043 8
₹ 200

BABA:
The Devotees' Questions
Dr. C. B. Satpathy
ISBN 978 81 207 8966 1
₹ 150

The Loving God:
Story of Shirdi Sai Baba
Dr. G. R. Vijayakumar
ISBN 978 81 207 8079 8
₹ 200

Sai Samartha and Ramana
Maharshi
S. Seshadri
ISBN 978 81 207 8986 9
₹150

Shirdi Sai Baba: The
Universal Master
Sri Kaleshwar
ISBN 978 81 207 9664 5 ₹ 150

The Age of Shirdi Sai
Dr. C. B. Satpathy
ISBN 978 81 207 8700 1
₹ 300

Message of Shri Sai
Suresh Chandra Panda
ISBN 978 81 207 9512 9
₹ 150

A Divine Journey with Baba
Vinny Chitluri
ISBN 978 81 207 9859 5
₹ 200

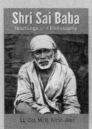

Shri Sai Baba
Teachings & Philosophy
Lt Col M B Nimbalkar
ISBN 978 81 207 2364 1
₹ 150

Baba's Divine Symphony
Vinny Chitluri
ISBN 978 81 207 8485 7
₹ 300

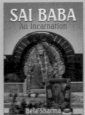

Sai Baba an Incarnation
Bela Sharma
ISBN 978 81 207 8833 6
₹ 200

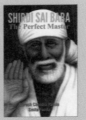

Shirdi Sai Baba: The Perfect Master
Suresh Chandra Panda & Smita Panda
ISBN 978 81 207 8113 9
₹ 200

The Eternal Sai Phenomenon
A R Nanda
ISBN 978 81 207 6086 8
₹ 200

Baba's Rinanubandh Leelas during His Sojourn in Shirdi
Compiled by Vinny Chitluri
ISBN 978 81 207 3403 6
₹ 200

Baba's Gurukul SHIRDI
Vinny Chitluri
ISBN 978 81 207 4770 8
₹ 200

Baba's Anurag
Love for His Devotees
Compiled by Vinny Chitluri
ISBN 978 81 207 5447 8
₹ 150

Baba's Vaani: His Sayings and Teachings
Compiled by Vinny Chitluri
ISBN 978 81 207 3859 1
₹ 200

The Gospel of Shri Shirdi Sai Baba: A Holy Spiritual Path
Dr Durai Arulneyam
ISBN 978 81 207 3997 0
₹ 150

Jagat Guru: Shri Shirdi Sai Baba
Prasada Jagannadha Rao
ISBN 978 81 207 8175 7
₹ 100

Spotlight on the Sai Story
Chakor Ajgaonker
ISBN 978 81 207 4399 1
₹ 200

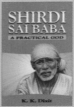

Shirdi Sai Baba
A Practical God
K. K. Dixit
ISBN 978 81 207 5918 3
₹ 75

Shri Sai Satcharita
The Life and Teachings of Shirdi Sai Baba
Translated by Indira Kher
ISBN 978 81 207 2211 8 ₹ 550(HB)
ISBN 978 81 207 2153 1 ₹ 450(PB)

Shirdi Sai Baba
The Divine Healer
Raj Chopra
ISBN 978 81 207 4766 1
₹ 150

Shirdi Sai Baba and other Perfect Masters
C B Satpathy
ISBN 978 81 207 2384 9
₹ 150

Sai Hari Katha
Dasganu Maharaj Translated by *Dr. Rabinder Nath Kakarya*
ISBN 978 81 207 3324 4
₹ 100

Unravelling the Enigma: Shirdi Sai Baba in the light of Sufism
Marianne Warren
ISBN 978 81 207 2147 0
₹ 400

I am always with you
Lorraine Walshe-Ryan
ISBN 978 81 207 3192 9
₹ 150

BABA- May I Answer
C.B. Satpathy
ISBN 978 81 207 4594 0
₹ 150

Ek An English Musical on the Life of Shirdi Sai Baba
Usha Akella
ISBN 978 81 207 6842 0
₹ 75

Sri Sai Baba
Sai Sharan Anand
Translated by V.B Kher
ISBN 978 81 207 1950 7
₹ 200

Sai Baba: His Divine Glimpses
V B Kher
ISBN 978 81 207 2291 0
₹ 95

**A Diamond Necklace To:
Shirdi Sai Baba**
Giridhar Ari
ISBN 978 81 207 5868 1
₹ 200

Life History of Shirdi Sai Baba
Ammula Sambasiva Rao
ISBN 978 81 207 7722 4
₹ 225

Shri Sai Baba- The Saviour
Dr. Rabinder Nath Kakarya
ISBN 978 81 207 4701 2
₹ 100

Sai Baba's 261 Leelas
Balkrishna Panday
ISBN 978 81 207 2727 4   ₹ 175

**A Solemn Pledge from
True Tales of Shirdi Sai Baba**
Dr B H Briz-Kishore
ISBN 978 81 207 2240 8   ₹ 95

God Who Walked on Earth:
The Life & Times of Shirdi Sai Baba
Rangaswami Parthasarathy
ISBN 978 81 207 1809 8   ₹ 200

**Shri Shirdi Sai Baba: His
Life and Miracles**
ISBN 978 81 207 2877 6
₹ 30

Shirdi Sai Baba Aratis
ISBN 978 81 207 8456 7
(English)   ₹ 10

Sree Sai Charitra Darshan
Mohan Jagannath Yadav
ISBN 978 81 207 8346 1
₹ 225

The Miracles of Sai Baba
ISBN 978 81 207 5433 1 (HB)
₹ 300

**The Thousand Names of Shirdi
Sai Baba**
Sri B.V. Narasimha Swami Ji
Hindi translation by
Dr. Rabinder Nath Kakarya
ISBN 978 81 207 3738 9   ₹ 75

**108 Names of
Shirdi Sai Baba**
ISBN 978 81 207 3074 8
₹ 50

**Shirdi Sai Speaks...
Sab Ka Malik Ek**
Quotes for the Day
ISBN 978 81 207 3101 1
₹ 200

Divine Gurus

Guru Charitra
Shree Swami Samarth
ISBN 978 81 207 3348 0
₹ 300

**Sri Swami Samarth
Maharaj of Akkalkot**
N.S. Karandikar
ISBN 978 81 207 3445 6
₹ 250

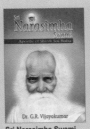

Hazrat Babajan:
A Pathan Sufi of Poona
Kevin R. D. Shepherd
ISBN 978 81 207 8698 1
₹ 200

**Sri Narasimha Swami
Apostle of Shirdi Sai Baba**
Dr. G.R. Vijayakumar
ISBN 978 81 207 4432 5
₹ 90

**Lord Sri Dattatreya
The Trinity**
Dwarika Mohan Mishra
ISBN 978 81 207 5417 1
₹ 200

श्री साई ज्ञानेश्वरी
राकेश जुनेजा
978 81 207 9491 7
₹ 250

साई ही क्यों?
राकेश जुनेजा
978 81 207 9610 2
₹ 200

जेल में साई साक्षात्कार
राकेश जुनेजा
978 81 207 9507 5
₹ 150

शिर्डी साई बाबा के ग्यारह अनमोल वचन
बेला शर्मा
978 93 85913 97 6
₹ 75

श्री साई सच्चरित्र
श्री शिरडी साई बाबा की अद्भुत जीवनी तथा उनके अमूल्य उपदेश
गोविंद रघुनाथ दाभोलकर (हेमाडपंत)
978 81 207 2500 3
₹ 350 (HB)

श्री साई चरित्र दर्शन
मोहन जगन्नाथ यादव
978 81 207 8350 8
₹ 200

साई सुमिरन
अंजु टंडन
978 81 207 8706 3
₹ 100

बाबा की वाणी-उनके वचन तथा आदेश
बेला शर्मा
978 81 207 4745 6
₹ 100

बाबा का अनुराग
विनी चितलुरी
978 81 207 6699 0
₹ 125

बाबा का ऋणानुबंध
विनी चितलुरी
978 81 207 5998 5
₹ 150

बाबा का गुरुकुल-शिरडी
विनी चितलुरी
978 81 207 6698 3
₹ 150

बाबा-आध्यात्मिक विचार
चन्द्रभानु सतपथी
978 81 207 4627 5
₹ 175

पृथ्वी पर अवतरित भगवान शिरडी के साई बाबा
रंगस्वामी पार्थसारथी
978 81 207 2101 2
₹ 200

साई बाबा एक अवतार
बेला शर्मा
978 81 207 6706 5
₹ 150

साई सत् चरित का प्रकाश
बेला शर्मा
978 81 207 7804 7
₹ 200

श्री शिरडी साई बाबा एवं अन्य सद्गुरु
चन्द्रभानु सतपथी
978 81 207 4401 1
₹ 90

साई शरण में
चन्द्रभानु सतपथी
978 81 207 2802 8
₹ 150

साई - सबका मालिक
कल्पना भाकुनी
978 81 207 9886 1
₹ 200

श्री साई बाबा के परम भक्त
डॉ. रबिन्द्रनाथ ककरिया
978 81 207 2779 3
₹ 125

शिरडी अंत: से अनंत
डॉ. रबिन्द्रनाथ ककरिया
978 81 207 8191 7
₹ 750